THE CAT
ENCYCLOPEDIA

ESTHER J. J. VERHOEF-VERHALLEN

THE CAT ENCYCLOPEDIA

KEY PORTER BOOKS

First published in The Netherlands by Rebo Productions Ltd.
Published in Canada in 1997 by Key Porter Books

Canadian Cataloguing in Publication Data

Verhoef-Verhallen, Esther J. J.
          The cat encyclopedia

Includes index.
ISBN 1-55013-892-8

1. Cat breeds — Encyclopedias.   2. Cats — Encyclopedias.
I. Title.

SF442.2.V47   1997a   636.8'003   C97-931481-X

The publisher gratefully acknowledges the support of the Canada Council for the Arts and the Ontario Arts Council for its publishing program.

Key Porter Books Limited
70 The Esplanade
Toronto, Ontario
Canada M5E 1R2

Cover design: Ton Wienbelt, The Netherlands
Production: TextCase, The Netherlands
Translation: Stephen Challacombe for First Edition Translations Ltd., Great Britain
Editing for the North American edition: Irene Cumming Kleeberg
Typesetting: Hof&Land Typografie, The Netherlands

98 99 00 6 5 4 3 2

Contents

Preface

People have always had the urge to classify their pets into different groups. While the hundreds of breeds of dogs can be classified fairly conveniently on the basis of their original uses, this is not true of cats. Cats have played an important role in the ancient religions of some cultures, and they have been held in high esteem all over the world for their prowess as hunters. While this is still the case in many countries, in the West the cat has increasingly assumed a new role – that of valued pet. Trying to classify cats according to their country or region of origin is also a fruitless task. The origins of some breeds can be traced back with a fair degree of certainty, but far more often there is little if any information available, and we can only guess at their exact origin on the basis of early writings and logical reasoning. What is more: a great many cat breeds have come about as a result of crosses or hybridization between existing breeds; these are therefore of mixed background. This is why in this encyclopedia of cats we have chosen a straightforward classification based on a physical characteristic that everyone can recognize: the length and type of coat. Because there are breeds that occur in both short- and long-haired varieties, the long-haired types of an originally short-haired breed have been dealt with separately. The principal aim of this encyclopedia is to give the reader the clearest possible idea of the different breeds in all their various guises. It is not possible to describe the breeds without using terms taken from genetics and the specific names given to coat colors and patterns, because these are in general use in cat fancy today. We have therefore tried in this book to describe the different colors and coat markings in a way that is clear to everyone. The genetic theory has also been dealt with as simply and accessibly as possible. In describing the breeds, we have not taken into account whether or not they are recognized by the numerous cat clubs and associations or the international organizations. Some breeds or varieties are recognized by one organization and not by another, or have been granted provisional recognition. If you are interested in a particular breed or variety, it makes sense to approach one or more associations about the breed or variety of your choice, so that you won't be confronted with any surprises after you have made your purchase.

If the information in this book assists readers in finding out whether the breed of their choice will fit into their home situation, and if they have increased their understanding of the various colors and coat patterns and the genetic background of the breed, this encyclopedia will have more than served its purpose.

Esther J.J. Verhoef-Verhallen

Left: Maine Coon

1   Things to consider

The life expectancy of a cat is some-where between ten and sixteen years; some cats can live considerably longer. Having a cat will affect your everyday life during that entire period. This is why it is so important to look beyond the attractions of having a cat as a pet and recognize the responsibility in-volved.

Practical considerations

Cats need daily attention. They must be combed or brushed, they need a good, varied diet, and the kitty litter will have to be cleaned at least once each day. Routine care obviously also includes keeping your pet free of fleas and worms, and you will have to take it to the vet regularly for vaccinations against a variety of feline diseases.

When you go on vacation, you will have to find someone who gets along with your cat (or cats) and is prepared to look after it (them) for you while you are away. If not, you will have to find a boarding cattery that has a good reputation and where your cat won't be too confined. And while we all hope it will

Persian Longhair, full color print

Left: Cats and dogs often get on very well together.

This Seal Point Siamese likes company.

never happen, cats, like people, do fall ill and have accidents, in which case the vet's bills can quickly add up to a considerable sum.

Most cats invite stroking because of their soft fur, but that same fur is shed all year round, which means that you will have to spend more time on housecleaning.

Some cats, particularly kittens, are clumsy and will break ornaments or knock over vases, and now and then your cat is almost certain to claw something you don't want him to, or cough up a hairball on the sofa or the new carpet... it's all part of having a cat as a pet.

It is important to understand this before you bring a kitten or an adult cat into your home.

Persian Longhairs need a lot of grooming.

Sphynx kittens

Which is the best breed for you?

When you set out to get a pedigree cat, you will inevitably base your initial choice on looks. There is nothing wrong with this approach, provided you bear in mind that pedigree cats not only have a breed-related appearance, but also have their own specific requirements when it comes to the care of the coat. What is more: different breeds have very different characteristics.

Some breeds are extremely active and playful while others are very placid. Individual members of some breeds will be perfectly happy to be left to their own devices while other breeds demand a great deal of attention and want to be the center of attention all the time.

Turkish Angora

Although the differences in character between the various breeds of cats are less marked than those between dog breeds, you must still be aware of them if you are to make the right choice. Otherwise you may find yourself regretting your decision, perhaps because you underestimated the amount of attention the animal would need, perhaps because it proves to be extremely playful and excitable, or the very opposite: too placid.

While the cat is still young, most people will find everything it does charming and attractive, but when they realize that caring for their Persian Longhair's coat is a time-consuming ritual that must be performed every single day, or when their elegant Siamese persistently demands attention at the top of his raucous voice, the pleasure can turn to irritation, and this is a shame.

This encyclopedia is therefore not confined to the outward characteristics of the breeds but also describes in so far as possible the typical breed character traits and discusses the question of how much care a particular breed needs and what this entails.

Even armed with this information, you would still be wise to go and look at the various breeds at a couple of cat shows before you take the plunge. Take the opportunity to talk about the breed to the breeders and enthusiasts there so that you can get a really clear idea of what it is like.

A kitten or an older cat

Most people will choose a kitten in preference to an older cat – often because they want the fun of seeing their new companion grow up, but sometimes also because they think that an older cat will not settle down in a new living environment. In practice, however, older cats can adapt to new situations just as easily as kittens and the bond you establish with an older cat will usually be just as close.

Some people opt for a kitten because they believe that a kitten is like a blank sheet of paper and that they can train it as they wish. However, a cat's character is determined in part by genetic factors, and in part by the environment in which it is raised as a kitten and the way it was treated by the breeder. The new owner's efforts will have some effect in the long run, but a kitten's character is essentially already established by the time you bring it home. The most you will be able to do is to teach the animal your house rules and polish some aspects of its character. A young

Sphynx kittens

The bond of trust you establish with an adult cat can be just as strong as that experienced with a kitten.

kitten will not automatically know what is and is not allowed in your home, and you will have to invest time in your new companion in order to teach it all the things it needs to know. For some people, a somewhat older cat that has already acquired a good basis elsewhere could therefore be a better choice. This will all depend very much, of course, on the background.

Many of the cat clubs and breed associations have a service that can put you in touch with people who for some reason have to or want to get rid of their cat.
Your local animal protection agency will also know people who specialize in rehousing specific breeds. These people will be completely candid with you because they have the interests of the breed at heart, and no one benefits if the rehousing endeavor ends in disappointment. People often think

The first meeting between two new companions.

that the animals involved are problem cats, but this is seldom the case. Personal circumstances, such as a divorce or a transfer abroad, can mean that someone has to part with a dearly loved pet. There are, however, cases where a cat has to be rehoused because it is aggressive or excessively timid, persistently sprays in the house, cannot or will not adapt to other pets, or has developed some other annoying character trait that makes it trying to live with. If you are considering taking on an older cat and you don't know enough about cats yourself, it is a good idea to take someone with you who has more experience with cats than you do and can give you advice and assistance.

A male or a female

The character differences between males and females are not as great as some people think, but generally speaking, males - neutered or otherwise - are likely to have a slightly more placid temperament than females.
The difference in appearance is much more apparent in most breeds. As a rule, the males are bigger and stockier than females and have an impressive, broad head.

If you are not planning to breed from your pedigree cat, whether you decide on a male or a female will be entirely a matter of personal preference. However, if you do not want to rule out the possibility of breeding you should choose a female. Because of their tendency to spray, whole toms are effectively impossible to keep indoors, and keeping one or more males as stud in an outdoor run involves a whole series of specific problems that you should not underestimate.

The scope of this book does not extend to this area, but you can always ask the advice of experienced breeders who will be able to give you a great deal of information. There are all sorts of reasons why it really is not a good idea for a beginner to start off with a breeding male.
With a good queen, you will be able to find a good selection of suitable studs and you will have more choice than if you keep your own tom.

If you have no ambitions to breed from your pedigree cat, the best thing to do, whatever its sex, is to have the animal neutered (you will find more information about this in Chapter 2 under the heading 'Birth Control'). Unlike dogs, which are excluded from shows if they are neutered, cats can be entered in special classes for neutered animals at cat shows, and there are prizes and titles to be won.

If you already have a pet

Cats generally fit in fairly well in a household where there are already pets in residence. If the dog is used to cats and treats them with respect, it will usually accept the newcomer too. Some dogs will chase cats when they are out but wouldn't dream of touching a hair on their 'own' cat's head. You must know your dog well to judge how it is likely to react to a cat. It goes without saying that if you are in any doubt, you should not leave the dog and cat alone together in the beginning. You should also make sure that the cat always has places to take refuge where the dog cannot follow. It may sometimes be easier to take in an older cat that is already used to dogs. Squealing, playful kittens on the run can sometimes be too much of a temptation for a dog, but in most cases the two animals will adjust to the new situation within a few weeks.

If you already have one or more cats, they may act insulted at first and refuse to accept the newcomer. However, they usually resolve their disagreements after a few months. There are, of course, always exceptions.

Some cats will simply never accept a newcomer and may express this by urinating or defecating in the house, becoming hypersensitive, withdrawing to a quiet part of the house and going off their food, or conversely by attacking the intruder at every available opportunity. Sometimes these differences are reconciled after a while, but there are cases – albeit rare – when a new home has to be found for one of the cats.

You sometimes hear that a kitten is more easily accepted, but you should not let this deter you from getting an adult animal. There are plenty of examples of cats who have developed firm friendships at an older age. Like people, cats may get on very well together or they may take an instant dislike to each other – it is almost impossible to tell in advance which way the scale will tip.

When you first bring the newcomer home, it is a good idea to let it get used to its new surroundings for a few hours before you introduce it to the other pets in the family. Relations with small birds such as parrots or canaries can pose a problem, but need not necessarily cause difficulties. A lot depends on the temperament of the cat and your own common sense.

Find a safe place for the bird cage so that the cat is not given the opportunity to misbehave. The same applies, of course, to small mammals such as hamsters, guinea pigs and rabbits, and to fish. You must remember that your new companion is a predatory animal and very few of them can really be trusted with small pets that would normally be their natural prey.

Cats and children

Many pets are originally acquired because the children are so keen to have them – and there is nothing wrong with that. It is very good for a child's social development to grow up with animals; it helps to teach them responsibility for other living creatures. However, you can never assume that your children, particularly

Teach children respect for cats.

if they are very small, will look after the cat themselves. Most children's sense of responsibility is not that great and for many of them the novelty soon wears off, so that it will ultimately be you who has to take care of the cat. Given the relatively advanced age that cats can reach, it is by no means impossible that the children will have left home while the cat is still in the prime of life. In other words, never get a cat just to keep the kids happy; you must want a cat yourself.

Teach your children that the cat is a living creature they must respect and that kittens – and adult cats, too, for that matter – should never be disturbed while they are sleeping.

Obviously you should not let your children treat their pet roughly or chase it around the house. This can make such a lasting impression on a cat that, depending on its character, it can turn aggressive out of fear or become incurably timid.

Lonely cats

Some people choose a cat as a pet because cats can be left at home alone more easily than dogs – and generally speaking this is true. You don't have to take a cat out for a walk and you can stay away overnight now and then without the cat suffering.

The cat's rather independent nature has, however, meant that it has been given the dubious label of 'solitary', and sadly this is often taken far too literally.

Many cats spend their days in loneliness and are seriously affected by it, since they really do need social contact. If you are not able to be around enough of the time yourself, consider getting two cats so that they can keep each other company while you are out.

Many cats do not do well if they are left alone. If you get two kittens, they will be able to keep each other company.

2 Caring for your cat

General grooming

With the exception of Sphynxes and Rex cats, all cats are blessed with a fur coat, thick or thin, which will shed to some extent all year round. In spring and early summer, however, you will find that a significant proportion of the coat will be shed. If you take good care of your cat's coat, you will be able to cut down substantially on the amount of hair that gets on to your furniture and carpeting. Weekly brushing is usually enough to keep a short-haired cat's coat in good condition. Most semi-longhairs also do not require a great deal of grooming. Caring for a Persian Long-hair's coat, however, is a very different matter. The texture of the Persian's long coat means that it will start to become matted within a very few days if you do not take proper care of it. If the coat is neglected for any length of time, the cat may suffer skin irritation and rashes, and may even develop bald patches and abscesses. If you are not prepared to spend a significant amount of time grooming your cat every single day, you should choose one of the less laborious and time-consuming breeds. The most suitable brushes and combs to use will depend on the texture and length of the coat of the

Persian Longhair, chinchilla

particular breed. Ask your kitten's breeder to show you the grooming equipment he or she uses, so that you can buy the same things. You will find that it will take you far less time to groom your cat, and you will do it much more effectively, if you use the right equipment.

People who show their cats not only groom them regularly, but also shampoo them every now and then. Most show cats are used to this and do not make a fuss. Even if you are not planning to show your cat, you may occasionally have to give it a bath. If you do this for the first time when your cat is older, neither you nor the cat will enjoy the experience, so it makes sense to accustom your cat to the procedure while it is still young,

Sphynx

even if it does not actually need to be bathed. When you are washing the cat, make sure water does not get into its eyes or ears and that it cannot swallow any.

Always use a special cat shampoo and never one intended for humans, because these can cause considerable damage to the texture of the coat and the sebaceous glands in the cat's skin. You can dry the cat with a hair dryer, but if this frightens it, you can rub it dry with a towel and leave it in a warm place free of drafts to finish drying up.

Some cats will continue to resist a bath. In this case, you can clean the coat with a special unscented powder that absorbs dirt and excess grease. Sprinkle the powder into the coat and massage it in well. Brush it out, and keep brushing until there is absolutely no trace of powder left in the coat. If you want to show your cat, you will have to groom it particularly meticulously. Cat shows are beauty contests, and a well-groomed animal will always do better than a cat whisked straight out of the garden and off to the show.

Care of the claws

Cats sharpen their claws frequently. This is instinctive behavior and you cannot stop a cat from doing it.

Kittens will sometimes sharpen their claws on the sofa or the door frame. Although you obviously have to discourage this, you cannot blame a kitten for it. Cats are animals and have no concept of the value of your posses-

Cats need to sharpen their claws regularly.

This Scottish Fold kitten is sharpening its claws on a scratching post.

sions. Make sure that your cat has its own scratching post or something like a sisal or coconut fiber mat. If you hold your kitten's forepaws and make scratching movements with them on the scratching post, it will usually get the idea pretty quickly.

It is good practice to clip off the sharp tips of the claws regularly, particularly on the forepaws – and remember the dew claw.

Always use good nail clippers or 'guillotine' type claw clippers. Most good pet shops stock these clippers and they are also sold at cat shows. If you do not feel comfortable about cutting your cat's claws yourself, ask your vet to do it whenever you take the cat in for any reason.

Care of the ears

Most cats go all their lives without suffering from any ear problems, and without their owners ever having cleaned their ears. Your cat may, however, occasionally be troubled by ear mites. The tell-tale signs are particles of dark brown, offensive-smelling matter. Ear mites must always be treated, otherwise they can cause severe ear infections. Your vet will have an effective remedy for ear mites available.

Use only an ear cleanser specially formulated for cats. Put a few drops of the ear lotion into the ear, massage, and then remove the lotion very gently using a tissue or cotton swab. Take great care when doing this, however, because you could push the dirt further into the ear where it will accumulate.

As with so many other things: if your kitten becomes accustomed to this at an early age, it will present few problems later.

Care of the eyes

Unless your cat belongs to one of the flat-faced breeds, you will seldom if ever need to clean its eyes. A bit of dirt in the corners of the eyes is easily removed with a soft, damp tissue. Flat-faced cats, such as Persians and Exotics, often need more eye care. Details of

Maine Coon

Check your cat's teeth regularly for signs of tartar.

how you should go about this are given under the headings for the individual breeds elsewhere in this book.

Care of the teeth

You should check the teeth regularly for tartar, because this dark deposit on the teeth can lead to decay and ultimately to tooth loss. Try to prevent tartar build-up by giving your cat hard, dry food on a regular basis. Never give your cat bones to chew because bones can splinter.

A cat's teeth and the shape of its mouth, unlike a dog's, are not designed to cope with bones. If your cat does have tartar, the best thing is to ask your vet to remove it.

Cats shed their milk teeth between three and six months of age, and it is good practice to check this process every now and then. A milk tooth that refuses to come out will cause the permanent tooth to come through crooked. Always consult your vet if in doubt.

Diet

Cats need more meat in their diets than dogs, and although some of them do develop strange eating habits, most cats will turn their noses up at cereal products and the like.

Some people prefer to make up their cat's food themselves, but this calls for a great deal of knowledge and understanding of both the cat's dietary requirements and the composi-

17

Cats can be finicky eaters.

tion of the various ingredients. Over the years many types of commercial cat food have been developed, the quality of which is guaranteed. When you feed your cat with these foods, you know that it is getting all the nutrients it needs.

The advantage of dry food is that it does not spoil quickly. This means that, unlike canned food or fresh meat, you can leave a bowl of it down for your cat all day, even in hot weather. You could therefore decide to give your cat dry food in the morning and to feed it in the evening with canned food, cooked meat such as chicken, turkey, rabbit or beef, or cooked and boned fish, such as cod and tuna. Lamb's heart is also very good for cats. Other types of offal, such as the lungs and stomach, are not suitable for cats because they need a lot of high-grade animal protein which is found primarily in muscle tissue. Whatever you do, you must make sure that your cat gets all the nutrition it needs, and you can really only be certain of this if you feed it not just meat and fish but also a good brand of canned or dry food too.

Choose a brand that does not contain artificial preservatives, because some cats are allergic to them. Cats should never be given pork because it can be infected with bacteria that causes Aujeszky's disease, which is fatal to cats.

Many cats love milk, but milk intended for human consumption is not good for cats and may cause diarrhoea. This is because many cats are unable to digest lactose, which is found in all dairy products that are not sterilized. In addition, the fat content of milk for humans is too low for cats. Full-fat evaporated milk or sterilized cream are good alternatives if you want to give your cat a treat every now and then. Pet food manufacturers are now also marketing milk designed especially for cats. It is not a good idea to give cats eggs, because cats have difficulty digesting them and raw eggs may contain bacteria.

Most cats will not eat more than they need, so you can feed them when they ask, but be careful with neutered cats of either sex. They are likely to develop an unsightly, sagging belly if they eat more than is good for them and do not get enough exercise.

Some cats are extremely finicky about what they eat. This may be the result of their having been given too monotonous a diet when they were kittens, so that they did not get used to different types of food, or it may be because they are spoiled. Your cat must always have access to clean drinking water, which you should change at least once a day.

Eating grass

Cats are fastidious animals and will wash themselves several times a day. Because the cat's tongue is covered with tiny, backward-facing hooks, the animal has no choice – it must swallow all the loose hairs that come out during grooming. A cat that is allowed outdoors will occasionally eat a few blades of

Grass is a natural emetic that helps the cat to bring up hairballs.

Cats groom themselves several times a day.

fresh grass, and this acts as a natural emetic – excessive hair builds up in the stomach and can cause problems.

If your cat is confined to the house, grow a pot of grass yourself so that it has the means to get rid of hairballs. If there is no grass available the cat may well start chewing on your house plants and, aside from the fact that you would probably not appreciate this, many house plants are poisonous to cats. You can help prevent the build-up of hairballs by brushing and combing your cat more often when it is shedding heavily.

Experts are now saying that cats eat grass not just as an emetic but probably also because it contains folic acid, something the cat needs from time to time.

The kitty litter

Kitty litters are available in a wide range of models and prices. The least expensive are simply open trays, and these are the least practical. Cats instinctively bury their urine and faeces, and filling may fly in all directions during enthusiastic excavation work. Some careless kitty litter users consistently position themselves in the tray and then proceed to perform over the edge. A tray with a cover is consequently a wise investment: the ones with a flap over the entrance and an odor filter in the cover are the best of all. While they may be more expensive, they do confine the less pleasant smells inevitably associated with a kitty litter. The same applies to the filling itself.

There are numerous types on the market, but as a rule the more expensive brands are better and they generally work out to be less expensive in the long run than the low-price brands. The ideal litter fillings are the ones that form clumps almost as soon as the cat urinates. This clump is then easily removed, and the rest of the filling in the tray stays clean and dry. This means that it is seldom necessary to change the filling in the tray – all you need to do is fill it up.

Fleas

Even cats that never go outdoors may get fleas, because you or your visitors can unwittingly bring these tiresome parasites in with you. It is fairly easy to see whether your cat has fleas by examining the places fleas like to congregate – at the base of the cat's tail and on its belly. What you are looking for are flea droppings, which look like small, irregularly shaped blackish specks.

Fleas can drive you and your cat mad. They multiply unbelievably fast. If the conditions are right, it takes only a few weeks for a couple of insignificant fleas to become a real plague in your home.

There are all sorts of flea control products on the market: some of them are simply useless, while others are extremely effective. Generally speaking, the flea powder you can get from your vet works very well. Flea collars – like ordinary collars – have the disadvantage of damaging the fur on the cat's neck, while the drawback of aerosols is that some cats are frightened by the noise. If you want

Fleas can cause your cat considerable irritation.

to remove the fleas by hand, you will need a small, fine-toothed comb.

As well as using a good flea treatment on the cat itself, it is crucial to treat the surroundings. Research has revealed that at any given time no fewer than 99 percent of fleas – in egg, larval or pupa stage – are not actually on the cat itself but in your home.

Frequent vacuuming is essential and you must not forget to treat your other pets as well. You should not use any of the flea preparations designed for adult cats on kittens, because they are very potent and can be dangerous to young animals. A flea powder specially formulated for kittens is the safest and most effective.

Worms

Worms are very nasty parasites which, if left unchecked, can cause serious physical damage to your cat. There are various types of worms, the most common of which are the roundworm and the tapeworm.

Most kittens are already infested with roundworm larvae at birth that have been passed on to them by the queen. This is impossible to prevent and it makes absolutely no difference whether or not the mother cat has been wormed regularly. This is why kittens will generally have been wormed by the breeder at an early age, and the treatment should be repeated before they go to their new owners. Preventive treatment twice a year usually provides sufficient protection for an adult cat.

Vaccinations

All cats should be vaccinated at regular intervals against a number of fatal or potentially fatal diseases, such as feline panleucopenia, feline calicivirus and cat flu. As long as kittens are being fed by the queen, they will be adequately protected against a number of diseases by the antibodies in her milk. Once they are weaned, however, it is time for them to be vaccinated. They will usually be given their first vaccination at around eight or nine weeks of age.

The vet will provide a vaccination booklet for every kitten he or she vaccinates, showing when the kitten was vaccinated, against which diseases and with which vaccines. It will also specify when the booster vaccinations are needed. Make sure you always keep your cat's vaccinations up to date, because prevention is better than cure.

Symptoms of illness

It is to be hoped that your cat does not fall ill. If you get your kitten from a reputable breeder, look after it well and feed it a varied diet, it is unlikely that you will have any problems. Things can, however, go wrong despite your best efforts.

This book does not set out to cover all the ailments from which a cat can suffer, but a list of symptoms that may or may not indicate a problem will perhaps be of help if you are concerned about your cat's health. This list is far from complete; the golden rule must always be to contact the vet if you have any doubts.

Signs of illness include:

- Diarrhea (not in all cases)
- Difficulty in passing water or constipation
- Urine or stools of an unusual color
- Third eyelid visible
- Discharge from the nose and eyes or from the vulva in the case of a female
- Raised temperature
- Sudden incontinence for no apparent reason
- A change in eating habits (eating more or less, drinking more)
- A change in behavior (very quiet, withdrawn, nervous)
- Skin rash
- Sudden hair loss or bald patches
- Drooling
- The cat stops grooming itself
- Weight loss

- Generally poor condition
- Swollen belly
- Difficulty walking
- More frequent vomiting of food (not to be confused with bringing up hairballs)

Birth control

Unless you are planning to keep your tom for stud purposes or to let your queen have a litter of kittens, it is best to have the cat neutered. Neutered males do not spray in the house and are far less likely to wander far from home. Un-neutered females (particularly the Oriental breeds) come into heat almost without warning and will then take advantage of every unguarded moment to get out. It is often virtually impossible to stop a queen from escaping.

Since the world is full of non-pedigree kittens for which it is extremely difficult to find good homes, it is irresponsible to 'just let' your cat have a litter.

If you are not sure about whether you want your cat to have a litter, the vet has drugs available to suppress oestrus temporarily. Spaying (neutering) is an irreversible surgical procedure. If they are going to have kittens at all, queens should have had a litter before their second year – after this it becomes more difficult, so do not postpone spaying any longer than necessary.

There is, incidentally, no truth in the old wives' tale that cats should have had one

A female in heat

litter before they are spayed. If you do not already have a good home for every kitten in a litter, you should not contemplate allowing your cat to breed.

Another point to bear in mind is that cats can contract an Aids virus similar to that found in humans. The virus is spread in the same way as it is in humans, and feline Aids, like human Aids, is incurable. Feline Aids cannot be transmitted to humans.

Cats, like humans, can also suffer from a viral form of leukemia. This likewise cannot be communicated to humans. Cats contract the disease through direct contact such as mating, washing and fighting.
Like feline Aids, it is always fatal. There are currently no good preventive vaccinations against these diseases. Responsible breeders always have their cats tested for these viruses before mating.

Housing

Most people do not let their pedigree cats roam freely outdoors because there is always a risk that they may be stolen. All outdoor cats also run a by no means negligible risk of being run over, injuring themselves in some other way, picking up poison or catching a disease. And obviously a tom or queen that has not been neutered should never be allowed to go out unattended!

A real paradise for cats: in this garden a curved-top fence and an electric wire keep the cats in.

A balcony enclosed with wire netting lets the cats get a breath of fresh air.

If you do not want to run any risks with your cats, a cat run is an ideal way for your cat to get a breath of fresh air. If you build the run so that it connects to a window or door, the cat can go in and out as it pleases. Other people secure their gardens so that it is very difficult for the cats to get out. A low-voltage wire strung along the top of the fence or a high fence curved inward at the top is usually enough to deter most cats. If you have a balcony you can enclose it with wire netting so that the cat can go outside with no risk of falling. If you instal a cat flap in the balcony door, the cat will have access at all times. Modifications such as these are not inexpensive, but the DIY enthusiasts among us can do a lot with a bit of creativity and a small budget.

A cat can also be kept indoors without problems. Fit good, strong screens to the windows so that you can air your house without letting the cat out. Some people believe it is cruel to keep a cat shut in or in a run, but there are also many people who do not like the thought of their cats straying into other people's gardens and causing a nuisance.

The great majority of cats will adjust quite happily to indoor life, provided they are accustomed to it from kittenhood, and will not pine for the great outdoors – although this obviously will not apply in all cases. If your home is on the small side and you are unable to let the cat out, it is a good idea to choose a placid breed, or to make sure that you have a good-sized scratching and climbing post and plenty of toys so that the cat does not get bored.

Rearing your kitten

When you bring a kitten into your home, logically the young animal will not have any notion of your house rules. You will have to teach it yourself. Some cats are more amenable to this than others who may persist in their undesirable behavior. Many people do not want their cat to jump up on the kitchen

Cats love to play, so make sure they have plenty of toys.

A cat flap lets your cat decide for itself when it comes and goes.

counter or the table, or sleep in their bed with them, while others have no problem with this at all. Keep true punishment to a minimum and always think carefully about what you are doing. Smacking your cat – or worse – is likely to simply make it nervous, so that it will then avoid you. You can shout 'no!' in an angry tone, but there is a good chance in this case that the cat will only refrain from the unacceptable behavior when you are around. A well-aimed jet from a water gun, which the cat will not associate with your presence, will usually encourage it to refrain from unwelcome activities.

Young cats are playful creatures and although you must allow them some leeway, they should never be allowed to get into the habit of climbing up your trouser legs or lashing out at you. Teach a kitten not to play roughly by making it quite clear that this behavior is unacceptable.

Almost every kitten will become house trained very quickly without any assistance from you. As soon as you get your kitten home, show it where the litter tray is. Start by using the same brand of litter as the breeder was using, so that it is familiar to the kitten. It will know what to do, and you should never have any accidents.

Verband
Deutscher Katzenfreunde e. V.
BEST OF BEST

3 Buying a pedigree cat

Where should I buy my pedigree cat?

There is one place where you will meet breeders of every breed imaginable and their cats – and that is at a cat show. These events are often advertised in the media, but you can also get in touch with a cat club and ask whether any cat shows are planned in your area in the near future. At a cat show you will be able to get an idea of what is available and to chat with breeders and owners of all sorts of breeds. You can also approach some of the cat associations to find out if any of the members has a litter of kittens of the breed you are looking for. You will find the addresses of cat clubs and associations in the specialist cat magazines, which are widely available.

If you are not ruling out the possibility of showing your kitten later on, or possibly even breeding from her, it makes sense to find out more about the breed rather than to buy a kitten from the first source you hear about. By talking to various breeders, visiting some of them and joining a breed association, you will learn more about the breed of your choice and will have a much better idea of what you are doing.

Although the progenitors of a pedigree cat are on record, so that the appearance and character of the kittens can to some extent be predicted, no breeder can ever guarantee that your kitten will grow up to be a champion. He or she can only help you to select a kitten with an excellent blood line which displays the right color, coat texture and typical physical breed characteristics at an early age. Whether these qualities will develop in the right way remains a matter of luck, although it does depend in part on the way you care for the animal.

On the other hand, litters also contain kittens which the breeder can see very early on will never meet the breed standard. These kittens are usually sold as 'pet quality', for

Left: No breeder can ever guarantee that your kitten will grow up to be a champion.

British Shorthair kitten, chinchilla

slightly less than would otherwise be charged. If you are not interested in breeding or showing, but are looking for a pet that is just a tiny bit special, this type of kitten could be ideal. The tiny departures from the standard that make the cat unsuitable for a career in the show ring can often be imperceptible to a layman, and if you do notice them you will probably be enchanted by your cat's little flaws. Some breeders will insist that you sign a form promising to get a kitten 'with faults' neutered when the time is ripe, and the pedigree certificate will probably be endorsed 'no progeny to be registered'. This means the breeder can be sure that the faults in the animal he or she has bred will not be passed on to future generations.

Things to watch out for

The time has come. You go to a breeder to look at a litter of kittens. There are a number of things you should be looking out for. Most

Healthy kittens are playful and curious.

breeders will have several cats in the house and possibly in outdoor runs as well, but if the house is literally crawling with cats this is not a good sign.

Cats need care and attention, and if someone has too many cats they can never get the individual attention they need. Take note of whether the kittens come over to meet you. Physically and psychologically healthy kittens will regard your visit as a welcome change in their daily routine. They will be interested and trusting, and if they are wide awake they should give you a demonstration of their playful nature.

Kittens that are raised in a segregated area and have not had much contact with people will often be more reserved and can come across as rather nervous or aloof. Since kittens spend the most important phase of their lives with the breeder – that is the period during which, among other things, they become accustomed to people – it is important that the breeder devotes plenty of attention to his or her kittens and lets them grow up in the

midst of the family, so that when they are older they will react sensibly in a variety of situations and in encounters with other animals and people.

If you are happy with these aspects of their background, examine the kittens to see whether they look healthy. Discharge from the nose or eyes, dirty ears or traces of diarrhea are not good signs. Leave kittens with symptoms like these strictly alone

Persian Longhair

Persian Longhair

Many cats like to sleep together.

breeding regulations, issuing pedigrees and organizing cat shows. Broadly speaking, the cat fancy is concentrated in a number of regions – America, Canada and Japan, Western Europe, Eastern Europe and Russia, Australia, New Zealand and South Africa. These regions have one or more umbrella organizations with affiliated associations. Because cat breeders are no different from the rest of us, there are a great many different clubs and splinter groups.

The major umbrella organizations include the CFA (Cat Fanciers Association Inc.), which has the greatest number of affiliated associations in the United States, Canada and Japan; the TICA (The International Cat Association), which also operates in North America; the GCCF (Governing Council of the Cat Fancy), which is based in the United Kingdom, and the FIFe (Fédération Internationale de Feline), which has the most

Brindled Great Dane and a black smoke Semi-Longhair

because they may be suffering from a disease. Other indications that all is not well include swollen bellies and bald patches in the coat, which can have various unpleasant causes. In such cases, which happily are very rare, you should obviously not visit another cattery on the same day because of the risk of infection! And you should never choose the runt of the litter. There is usually a very good reason why this kitten is so much smaller and weaker than the rest.

A serious breeder will never let kittens go to their new owners until they are at least twelve weeks old and will always have had the sire and queen tested for feline leukemia and feline Aids, for which no 100 percent reliable vaccines have as yet been developed.

Cat Clubs

There are a great many cat clubs all over the world, whose activities include establishing affiliated associations in Europe, the Far East and South America. There are also many cat clubs in Europe that are not affiliated with any of the umbrella organizations. These are the 'independents'. As far as admitting one another's cats to their shows and recognizing breeds, however, they do tend to work together to some extent. There are various clubs that cooperate in South Africa. In Australia and New Zealand the idea of an umbrella organization has never really caught on – possibly because of the independent attitude of the people. There are a great many clubs and federations which sometimes work well together and sometimes do not.

Regarding the issue of which breeds and colors are fully recognized, there are differences not just between the umbrella organizations but also between associations. Generally speaking, the larger umbrella organizations are a bit more conservative when it comes to breed recognition than smaller or independent organizations. In this book, I have tried to include as many of the well-known and less familiar breeds as possible,

with illustrations of all sorts of different coat colors and patterns. I have not concerned myself with the question of whether the breed or the color is recognized by a particular association or organization. This encyclopedia is intended for people who are looking for the right breed of cat for them, and the illustrations give an impression of the colors found in the breed. If you plan to show your cat or would like to breed from it, you would be well advised to get in touch with at least one association to find out about the situation with the breed of your choice.

In this encyclopedia you will also find a number of fairly rare breeds, and it is by no means impossible that you would have to import a kitten of the breed you want from another country or even from another part of the world. Here again, the cat clubs should be able to help you. They can give you addresses and phone numbers of foreign cat associations that you can contact for information on breeders of the rare breed you are looking for. However, keep in mind that quarantine restrictions will apply.

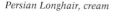

Persian Longhair, cream

4 Coat colors

Anyone who is unfamiliar with cats'
coat colors can find the names breeders
give the different shades very confusing,
so in this chapter we will try to explain
some of what is involved.
The descriptions of the various coat
colors and patterns are, however, not
altogether complete. We have chosen to
deal with the ones you are most likely
to come across.

Melanim

Cats' coat colors are created by tiny particles of pigment in the hairs. These particles can vary in shape, size and quantity.
These particles of pigment are known as
melanins. All of the colors found in cats de-
rive from just two types of 'basic melanin':
eumelanin causes a black coat color, and
phaeomelanin produces a red coat color.
When a mutation changes the shape of the
eumelanin, light is reflected back differently
and we see that the coat color is not black
but chocolate, for example, or cinnamon.
In the case of phaeomelanin these differences are not as visible as they are with
eumelanin; this is why the various shades of
red that can occur in cats' coats are referred
to simply as 'red'.

Dilution

A diluted color occurs if a number of
melanins are 'missing', therewith diminishing
the intensity of the color. Black becomes
blue, chocolate turns to lilac, and cinnamon
fades to fawn. The red color can also be
diluted; the coat color is then called cream.

Tabby

There are four different tabby patterns:
ticked, mackerel (striped), spotted and
classic (also known as blotched). In the

United States, a distinction is made between
the classic tabby (simply referred to as
Tabby), which is seen in both the mackerel
and spotted versions, and the patched tabby.
The patterns occur as a result of a particular
gene that suppresses pigmentation at different places in the hair, creating 'bands' in the
hair. (Perhaps the best example is the hair of
the ordinary wild rabbit.) If you look closely
at a tabby cat's coat, you will see that the
individual hairs have alternating bands of
gray-beige and black. The dark bands reveal
the real color of the coat.

A cat whose darkest color is blue and who
has a blotched pattern is known as a blue
classic tabby. The difference between a
mackerel and a spotted tabby pattern can
sometimes be only slight, because these two
patterns are caused by the same gene. A
spotted cat is actually a mackerel cat in
which the stripes are interrupted. Tabby cats
are also sometimes referred to as agouti cats,
because in fact every cat carries a gene for a
particular tabby pattern, but this pattern is
only visible to us if the cat also carries an
agouti gene. A cat with no tabby markings in
its coat is known as a non-agouti cat.
Red and cream cats always have more or less
of a tabby pattern in their coats – even those
cats who do not carry an agouti gene – and
this can sometimes lead to confusion.
According to the classification applied by the
CFA, the largest association of breed organ-

Chocolate Spotted Oriental Shorthair

izations in the United States, a cat with patches of red and/or cream or with two different colors on its nose leather and/or paw pads will be classified as a silver, blue or brown patched tabby, depending on the real color of the coat.

Tortoiseshell

Tortoiseshell is also often referred to as tortie. Tortoiseshell cats are almost always female. A tortoiseshell coat contains both eumelanin and phaeomelanin – in other words, the cat has a combined black and red coat color, but the coat could equally easily be chocolate and red or cinnamon and red. Diluted tortoiseshell is also very common. In this case the coat is blue and cream, lilac and cream or fawn and cream. Sometimes the amount of eumelanin dominates the phaeomelanin. The cat will then be almost entirely black (or chocolate, cinnamon, blue, lilac or fawn)

with only a little red or cream. The patches of color can occur in large, clearly defined areas or they can be very small and merge into one another. Nevertheless this pattern is referred to as tortoiseshell. The basic color of the coat is always black or a derivative of black. A black and red tortoiseshell cat is called a Black Tortie and a cat with a lilac and cream tortoiseshell coat is called a Lilac Tortie. A tortoiseshell cat can also have a great many or a few white patches. This is known as Tortie and White.

Tortie Tabby

Tortie Tabby or Torbie cats have coats containing both eumelanins and phaeomelanins; in some places they also have hair with alternating light and dark bands. These are cats with both a tortoiseshell and a tabby pattern. A cat whose basic color (always a eumelanin) is chocolate, for example, but

Chocolate Tortoiseshell Oriental Shorthair

Black Striped Tortie and White Turkish Angora

Black Silver Classic Tabby British Shorthair

which has a tabby pattern visible here and there through the tortoiseshell patches, is described as a Chocolate Mackerel Tortie Tabby. If the cat also has white in its coat, it is known as a Chocolate Mackerel Tortie Tabby with White.

A tortoiseshell cat that only shows faint tabby markings in the red or cream colored patches is not a Tortie Tabby, because there is always a tabby pattern more or less visible in these coat colors, even if the cat does not carry an agouti gene. A cat is only described as a Tortie Tabby if the basic color (black, chocolate, cinnamon, blue, fawn or lilac) shows some tabby markings.

Colorpoints

Siamese and Birmans are among the breeds of cat that have a light color on the body and a face, ears, legs and tail of a darker color.

This pattern is described as Colorpoint or sometimes Himalayan. The 'real' color of the cat is the dark color on its extremities or 'points'. These are the head, legs, tail and, in a male, the scrotum. The reason why the true color of the cat only appears in these areas is that these are the parts of the body where the

Black Spotted Tabby British Shorthair

temperature is lowest. In the case of partial albinism, which is what the point factor actually is, these are the only places where the color can come through.

A colorpoint can occur in any of the colors we have already discussed. The points can therefore be a solid color, but tortoiseshell, tortie tabby and tabby markings all occur frequently. Colorpoints always have blue eyes.

Silver

A cat whose undercoat is effectively white, which means that the individual hairs are white at the roots and only show the 'true' coat color halfway up or at the tip, is called Silver. Silver is caused by a separate gene (the inhibitor gene) that inhibits the pigmentation at the hair root to such an extent that the hair contains no pigment whatsoever at this point. There are various names for this phenomenon, depending on the amount of 'silver' in the cat's coat, the existence or lack of tabby markings and the 'true' color of the cat. You will find these names, where applicable, in the breed descriptions. The inhibitor gene can occur in conjunction with all sorts of colors and color patterns.

The cat's 'true' coat color is the color on the tips of the hair. A Tortie Tabby cat whose basic coat color is black, with a more or less pronounced classic tabby pattern and a white silver undercoat, is described as a Black Silver Classic Tortie Tabby.

White

One of the oldest colors for the domestic cat is solid white. For centuries, people have been fascinated by this particularly attractive coat color. In Turkey a white cat with one amber and one blue eye is regarded as a harbinger of good fortune. Devout Turks believe that their beloved leader Ataturk will be reincarnated in the form of an odd-eyed white cat. In medieval Europe, the white cat – unlike his black cousin – was also thought to be lucky. White in the cat occurs in different forms, which we will look at now.

DOMINANT WHITE
The white coat color is almost always caused by a dominant gene. You should visualize this as a sort of blanket, masking the cat's actual color.

A white cat does not show its real color; there are no pigment cells in the hair shaft. The dominant gene that causes this prevents pigment from being produced. White cats' eyes are seen in a range of colors. The most common eye colors are gold and green. The 'odd-eyed' form, with one blue eye and one gold or green eye, is much rarer, while the rarest of all is the pure white cat with two blue eyes.

Extreme care is needed when breeding white cats, whatever the breed, because a small proportion of white cats are deaf. This is related to the absence of pigment in the hair, because the inner ear of the cat also contains hairs that vibrate when sound waves enter the ear. If the pigment is missing from these hairs they are not stiff enough to be set in motion. As a result, the sound signal is not passed on to the auditory nerve and therefore never reaches the brain.

Fortunately, most white cats still do have pigment in the hairs in the inner ear. It is highly inadvisable to breed from two white cats because the risk of deaf offspring is very considerable – and obviously no one should ever breed from deaf white cats.

OTHER WHITE CATS
Another white gene is occasionally found in cats. It causes the blue-eyed albino. This inherited characteristic is passed on through a recessive gene. It occurs primarily in cats from the Far East and is also present in a number of Siamese blood lines – mainly American ones. The true red-eyed albino has so far not been found in the domestic cat.

5 Genetics

Most breeders waiting for a litter from a particular pairing will be able to tell you in advance what colors the kittens are likely to be and whether they will be long- or short-haired. These breeders are not clairvoyant, they have simply learned something about feline genetics. Characteristics like coat color and coat length, build, conformation, and a great many other features are inherited, and when the breeder is familiar with the characteristics of the kittens' progenitors a fairly straightforward probability calculation can be made.

This encyclopedia uses various genetic terms, and you will only be able to understand them if you know a little about genetics. We have consequently included this short chapter to cover the basics. Genetics is not as difficult as you might think; once you understand the basic principles you are already well on the way!

Basic genetics

A cat has nineteen pairs of chromosomes in every single cell in its body. This is where the genetic information is stored. The only exceptions to this are the egg cells in the female and the sperm cells in the male. These cells contain nineteen single chromosomes—each is the random half of a pair of chromosomes. This makes sense, because when the egg and the sperm fuse together, the nineteen single chromosomes from the female and the nineteen single chromosomes from the male join together to form the pairs of chromosomes that together contain all the hereditary characteristics needed to create a cat. This

means that a kitten gets half of the tom's genetic characteristics and half of the queen's. These genes do not mix–nature has seen to that. Mixing would mean that a cross between a red cat and a white cat would produce cream kittens, and a longhair and shorthair cross should result in a litter of semi-longhairs. This is not what happens, however, because some genes are dominant and others are recessive.

Dominant means that this characteristic dominates and will always show up in the appearance of an individual cat carrying that gene. Recessive means that the characteristic only emerges if it is not suppressed by a dominant gene. If a recessively inherited characteristic is to emerge, the kitten will have to get the same recessive gene from both its father and its mother.

This cat has two recessive characteristics – the blue coat color and the long-haired coat

Left: Black and White Maine Coon

35

Norwegian Forest Cat kittens

AN EXAMPLE

A simple example will help to explain how this works. The black coat color, indicated by a capital D, is dominant over the blue coat color, indicated by a small d. If we were to mate a purebred black tom (DD) with a purebred blue queen (dd), the kitten would get a single dominant gene for black (D) from its father and a recessive gene for blue (d)

Silver Tabby British Shorthair

from its mother. Because the dominant gene always overrides a recessive one, the kitten will have a black coat, but it will carry not only the dominant gene for black (which everyone can see), but also the recessive gene for blue that it has inherited from the queen. This kitten's genetic code is consequently Dd. Now we can theoretically mate this kitten with his litter sister, who carries the same combination of genes (Dd) for coat color. The kittens from this mating will also get a random half of the chromosome pairs from each parent. This means two dominant genes, two recessive genes or a dominant and a recessive gene can come together.

Because a different combination can occur in each fusion of an egg and a sperm cell, the following colors can be expected from this cross:

• One or more of the kittens can inherit the recessive gene for a blue coat color from both parents: the kitten will be blue and the genetic code will be dd.

• One or more of the kittens can inherit the dominant gene for black from both parents: the coat color will be black and the genetic code will be DD.

• One or more of the kittens can inherit the recessive gene for blue from one parent and the dominant gene for black from the other. These kittens will always have black coats, because the dominant gene for black will prevail, but they carry the gene for blue and will be able to pass it on to future generations. The genetic code of these animals is Dd.

As a rule, you would expect to get more black than blue kittens in a litter like this one, but it is by no means impossible for there to be no blue kittens at all. However, we can only work out the probabilities on the basis of the genetic codes for color, markings and coat length.

In terms of percentage, the chance of black kittens carrying two genes for black resulting from this combination is 25 percent, the chance of black kittens that carry both the gene for black and the gene for blue is 50 percent and the chance of blue kittens, which of course carry two genes for blue, is again 25

The virtual absence of hair is caused by a recessive gene

percent. Once you have grasped the principle of the thing, you can start to make your own simple probability calculations. You do, however, need to know which characteristics in the cat are dominant and which are recessive. The list below tells you which is which.

Dominant and recessive characteristics

The characteristics in the left-hand column are dominant over the characteristics in the right-hand column.

Hair type:

short hair	long hair
normal coat	hairless
normal coat	curly coat (Devon and Cornish Rex)
wiry coat	normal coat
curly coat (Selkirk Rex)	normal coat

Colors:

self colors	Burmese, Tonkinese and Siamese markings
black	blue
black	chocolate
red	cream
chocolate	lilac
chocolate	cinnamon
cinnamon	fawn
white markings	completely colored
white (depending)	all other colors

Patterns and markings:

tabby marking	solid color
ticked tabby	all other tabby patterns
mackerel or spotted tabby	classic tabby
silver-white undercoat	coat colored throughout

Physical characteristics:

folded ears	upright ears
short legs	normal legs
short or absent tail (Manx, Kuril Bobtail)	complete tail
complete tail	very short tail (Japanese, American and Kuril Bobtail)

Not all of the cat's characteristics are passed on in as clearly a dominant or recessive form as those outlined above. Some dominant characteristics, for example, will only show up in the cat's appearance if there is another gene present to activate that specific gene, while other characteristics are gender linked.

If this short description has aroused your interest in genetics, you might like to know that there are many books on the subject. There is also a glossary at the back of this encyclopedia, containing definitions of some of the terms used.

6 The development of pedigree cats

The very first reference to a pedigree cat is to the Angora, now known as the Turkish Angora.

As early as the seventeenth century, travellers to Turkey were bringing these cats back to Europe, where they soon became the cherished pets of many of the aristocratic and wealthy people of the age. There are now almost seventy breeds of this cat, in countless varieties and colors, thirty-three of which are registered with the CFA. How did all these different cats come to be?

The Jungle Cat

All domesticated cats are descendants of *Felix domesticus*, the domestic house cat of Ancient Egypt. Although scientists still have not been able to agree on this point, it is very probable that the Jungle Cat, a wild cat, is the ancestor of the first Egyptian house cats. The experts believe that the influence of the European Wild Cat is less likely, since this animal – unlike the Jungle Cat – is very difficult to keep in captivity, and even the young do not adapt to living with people.

Domestic cats were originally found only in Egypt and neighboring regions. Archaeological digs in Europe and America have never unearthed any evidence of a domesticated cat that lived in the vicinity of people in this period or earlier. The fact that the cats of Egypt spread throughout the world is primarily a result of man's wanderlust. Cats were taken on sea voyages to keep down the mice and rats on board ship, and when people emigrated to another country or another continent they took their favorite mousers with them so that the animals could continue to be of service in their new

Left: the Jungle Cat

surroundings. The Jungle Cat was originally a sand-colored animal with a short coat, but the cats of today come in an immense variety of colors and markings, with many different coat lengths and textures.

Their physical build also varies from one breed to another. If we look at the origin of the many breeds that now exist, we find that cats from the Orient tend to be slender, svelte and smooth-haired, while the larger and sturdier cats with a thicker coat are traditionally found in Europe.

Mutations

All these breeds with their different physical build and coat texture descend from a single ancestor. The fact that they are so different is the result of a series of mutations that have taken place over the centuries. Mutations are changes in genetic material that occur spontaneously. They occur regularly, not just in cats, but in everything that lives and reproduces.

The phenomenon is also found, for example, in viruses and plants. Mutations can change all sorts of different physical characteristics, which are not necessarily noticeable.

Some mutations, on the other hand, are obvious: an animal is born, for instance, with a coat in a color that has never occurred in that species before, or its tail is a different length from all the others. These are mutations that everyone can see. Since the mutation occurs in the animal's genetic material, the characteristic can be passed on to future generations.

If the mutation gives the animal an advantage over the other members of the species, the animal and its offspring have a greater chance of survival and hence a better chance of reproducing than the non-mutant members of the species.

Imagine, for example, a cat that must survive in a harsh climate. If it is blessed with a thick coat that does not become matted, the cat will undoubtedly have an advantage over cats with a thinner coat that tangles easily. If a mutation is a fortunate one, the effect will rapidly become evident in the whole population of that particular species.

The mutant's young, a number of whom will resemble their parent, share the advantage and in turn have a better chance of reproducing. Slowly but surely the animals with the new characteristic will get the upper hand over the animals that do not have it.

The outcome of a mutation may not always be beneficial. Sometimes the mutation may actually damage the individual's chances of survival. An animal born in that same harsh climate with no coat or with a very soft, long-haired coat that tangles easily will be at a disadvantage in relation to the other members of the species. The chances of a cat with

a long, thick coat surviving in the heat of the tropics are none too good, either. An animal like this would scarcely be able to keep itself alive, let alone reproduce. This harmful characteristic would also be passed on to subsequent generations. Mutations are a natural phenomenon and they give the species a better chance of survival in an ever-changing environment.

The cats from the ancient world were taken by man to all four corners of the world, where the animals went their own way and developed characteristics – enhanced by genetic changes – that made it easier for them to survive.

It is therefore by no means a coincidence that it is the short-haired breeds that come from the east, from areas where the climate is tropical, and that cats with a thick coat naturally occur in cooler climates.

Natural breeds

The term natural breeds is used several times in this encyclopedia. By this we mean groups of cats that appeared without any deliberate intervention by cat breeders and that have succeeded in maintaining their populations independently over the centuries.

The Norwegian Forest Cat, the Japanese Bobtail and the Turkish Van are good examples of natural breeds. Members of breeds like these are still found today in the countries or regions where they were first discovered. They differ little if at all from cats of the same breed are on view at shows. Enthusiasts of these breeds regularly return to the country or region of origin to look for individuals that might make a valuable addition to their catteries.

Several of the natural breeds have gained a devoted following, but there are still natural breeds that have not yet been discovered by the cat fancy or in which there seems to be little interest. Travellers who have visited Java often come back with stories of the numerous, slender native cats with striking bobbed tails. These animals live near towns

Silver Tabby British Shorthair

and villages, but so far no one has thought of breeding them systematically to preserve their specific common characteristics – unlike the Norwegian Forest Cat, the Manx, the Japanese Bobtail, the Turkish Angora and the Turkish Van, all breeds that are commonly seen at cat shows.

Where most breeders aim to develop cats with an even longer coat or an even richer color, the breeders of natural breeds have only one aim–to maintain the original appearance and character of the breed.

When the animals are created by breeders by means of crosses between breeds, the results are described as non-natural breeds. This term is also used for animals that do still occur in their native region, but whose show bench descendants differ so greatly from the original form as a result of selective breeding that no individuals that meet the current breed standard can be found in the original areas. The Siamese is a classic example of

this. The lean, rangy Siamese with their long, wedge-shaped heads that we see at shows today are far removed from the Siamese found in Thailand (formerly Siam), whose heads are much more rounded and conformation is considerably cobbier.

Creations

Not all cat breeds came about more or less by chance. There are a number of breeds that have been deliberately created by cat lovers. The Exotic, for example, is a breed created by crossing Persian with American Shorthair. The breeders' aim was – and is – to produce a breed that looks like the Persian Longhair but has a coat that requires very little care. The Bengal is another manufactured breed. It has the blood of both domestic pedigree cats and Felis bengalensis, the Asian Leopard Cat, flowing through its veins. The purpose of the exercise is to develop a pedigree cat with the

A Turkish Angora in its full winter coat

A Siamese from around the turn of the century

The Asian Leopard Cat is one of the forefathers of a new breed of cat.

looks of a wild cat but a docile nature. The British Shorthair and the Persian Longhair are also good examples of breeds that have been purposely created by breeders in one way or another. By continually selecting for the desired characteristics, such as the longest possible coat, or the shortest possible nose, the breeders ultimately produce an animal with its own individual breed-specific appearance.

Mutants

We have looked at the group of natural breeds, breeds that have developed over the years without the intervention of people, and the group of cats that have been deliberately and specifically bred to conform to a particular type. The breeds in the third group of cats are all based on one or more mutants with a striking physical characteristic – a virtually hairless skin, for instance, like the Sphynx, or folded ears like the Scottish Fold.

Unlike the natural breeds, these cats have been able to count on the care and attention of cat lovers from the outset.

The first Scottish Fold, for example, was the offspring of two farm cats and was born in a barn in Scotland. A number of people found this little tom so unusual and appealing that they decided to establish a breed and pass on the folded ears to subsequent generations. These animals would probably have managed to survive without human intervention, but since they were not given the opportunity this is something we will never know.

From alley cat to pedigree cat

People have been intrigued by cats for thousands of years. The Ancient Egyptians revered and worshipped cats, while in the Middle Ages they were feared and reviled. Whatever the nature of the response, cats have always fascinated people all over the world.
Cat fancy has a relatively short history. It did not really get off the ground until the late nineteenth and early twentieth centuries. A couple of hundred years earlier, the Angora, now known under the breed name Turkish Angora, was brought back to Europe from Turkey and the neighboring countries by merchants.

The Europeans were captivated by the look of these elegant white cats with their semi-long coats and blue eyes. Until this time people had only ever seen the short-haired farm cats and alley cats that kept the rats and mice down in barns and houses.

To the nobility of the time, the Angora was so different and so special in every respect that for a long time these cats were only ever seen in the castles and stately homes of the well-to-do, and they became all the rage at the French Court. In the nineteenth century, merchant sailors brought back more extraordinary cats from strange and distant lands.

The Siamese was one of them. These blue-eyed cats with their slender build and dark points were cherished and pampered by the sailors' wives back home in Britain. At that time it was mainly women who concerned themselves with cats. The men were away from home too often and for too long to bother about the fortunes of the animals. However, when they saw unusual cats on their travels they did attempt to capture them so they could take them home as presents for their wives.

Women and a handful of men who loved exotic cats started to correspond with one another about their animals, and it was not long before the first real cat show of any significance was staged. The year was 1871 and the venue was London's Crystal Palace. The show was organized by a man called Harrison Weir, a leading light of the cat fancy.

Keeping and breeding pedigree cats has long since ceased to be the prerogative of the rich. Nowadays there are cat lovers and cat breeders at every level of society, and interest in pedigree cats is growing all the time.

7 Short-haired breeds

British Shorthair

The British Shorthair is without a doubt the most popular short-haired pedigree cat in Europe. Its great adaptability means that the British Shorthair can live equally happily out in the country or in a top-floor apartment. Their equable temper and docile, friendly nature make them ideal pets for many people. Their looks are striking. With their round heads and large, expressive eyes, their stocky build and their extremely soft and dense coat, they resemble nothing so much as a teddy bear. They are bred in a great many colors and patterns, but the Blue British Shorthair is undoubtedly the most popular.

History

The British Shorthair originated in Great Britain around the turn of the century. At that time, well-to-do British people started showing exotic pedigree cats, which almost without exception came from Oriental countries.

The Siamese, the (Turkish) Angora and the forerunner of the Persian Longhair were particularly highly prized for their striking appearance. Many cat lovers of the period kept very ordinary house cats alongside the exotic breeds. In terms of beauty and color,

Young Blue and White Bi-color British Shorthair

these domestic cats were a match for any imported pedigree animal, but they were simply not considered to be 'interesting' as a breed.

Society consequently regarded these cats as very common. The type varied quite considerably because they had never been deliberately bred to bring out specific characteristics.

A number of cat lovers decided that the native English cats should also be involved in pedigree cat breeding so that they could act as a counterweight at shows to the usually fine-built Oriental short-haired breeds. A cat with the conformation of a sturdy Angora (the forerunner of the Persian Longhair), but with a short coat, was the ideal that the breeders were work-

Blue British Shorthair

Left: Blue British Shorthair kitten

45

Blue Silver Classic Tabby British Shorthair

British Shorthair kitten

ing towards. They selected their domestic cats for a compact, stocky build and crossed them with Persians to get the type they wanted. At first the breed, by then dubbed the British Shorthair, was bred primarily for a blue coat color, because this color was regarded as particularly chic at the time.

The British were not the only ones getting involved in breeding and showing cats. Interest in pedigree cats also began to grow in continental Europe, where breeders were also starting to breed exclusive pedigree breeds from their own domestic cats.

The cats of mainland Europe were of the same type as the cats being bred in Britain, but they were known as European, rather than British, Shorthairs. Because the two breeds were very similar and Angoras were regularly crossed with both the British and the European Shorthair, there was soon interaction between Great Britain and the Continent.

British Shorthair kittens at four weeks

At about the same time, people in Scandinavia were also involved in the selective breeding of short-haired domestic cats; they were shown as European Shorthairs, but the Scandinavian cats were of a very different type. In Scandinavia, unlike in other countries, the breeders tried to keep the cats as purebred as possible and crosses

A Blue British Shorthair from around the turn of the century.

A Black Tortie and White British Shorthair from around the turn of the century.

cats of the less stocky type have been known as European Shorthairs. From then on, the cats on the mainland of Europe were classified under the same name and breed standard as the British Shorthair – a logical step given their origins, breeding aims and appearance. While the (Scandinavian) European Shorthair has remained the farm cat it always was, in a very short span the British Shorthair has developed into a popular pedigree cat with a very distinctive appearance. Even today the breed is still occasionally crossed with Persian Longhairs to ensure that the British Shorthair does not lose type. This is not the only reason why the Persian Longhair has always been an important influence on the British Shorthair: the new colors that have been bred over the years also come from the Persian Longhair. While originally the breed was found only in blue, a few other self colors and tabby, nowadays the British Shorthair is being bred in many different colors and, in view of the recent intro-

A British Shorthair from around the turn of the century.

with Angoras (and later with Persian Longhairs) were forbidden. This gave rise to considerable confusion. Only one breed standard had been drawn up for the European Shorthair, but while the European Shorthairs bred in the Netherlands, Germany and elsewhere bore little resemblance to the Scandinavian cats, they were very like the British Shorthair. Nevertheless, the Scandinavians regularly imported British Shorthairs from Great Britain and exhibited them at shows. The two different breeds were consequently judged under the same breed standard.

None of this made much sense and so the Scandinavian breeders of the European Shorthair submitted a request to the FIFe (the leading cat breed organization in Europe), asking for permission to split the two types. The FIFe granted the request: since 1 January 1982 only the Scandinavian

Cream British Shorthair

Lilac Point British Shorthair

duction of the Colorpoint, Chocolate and Lilac, Chinchilla, Shaded Silver and Golden British Shorthair, the trend shows little sign of coming to an end.

Temperament

Cats of this breed are known for their equable and amiable temperament. Most British Shorthairs are extremely tolerant and friendly and they are highly adaptable. Until they are a year or two old, the kittens are as playful as any other cat, but after this most of them become less active and do not make their presence in your house felt in any intrusive way – it is not in their nature to vocally demand attention. British Shorthairs can keep themselves amused relatively well. Sometimes they will spend hours sleeping, but they also love being cuddled and stroked, and they definitely appreciate a lot of contact with the other members of the family. Despite their placid nature, British Shorthairs will not always put up with absolutely everything; they retain their own character and will certainly let it be known if they are displeased for any reason.

British Shorthairs usually get on well with other cats and similarly do well with dogs. Because they are good-tempered and gentle, most of them are very good with children. The only condition is that they be properly socialized, which means that you should only

ever get a kitten from a breeder who has raised the kittens in the family circle – but then this basically applies to all cats.

Care

The British Shorthair needs good grooming. Generally speaking, a weekly session with a pig-bristle brush is enough to keep the coat in good condition. When the cat is shedding, a special rubber brush is ideal for removing loose, dead hairs, but use it with care because you could inadvertently damage the coat if you are overly enthusiastic. You should only clean the ears if they are actually dirty. Use a

Lilac British Shorthair

British Shorthair kitten

special ear cleaner for cats, massage gently into the ear and then dab off with a tissue. You can also use cotton swabs, provided that you are aware of the danger of pushing the dirt further into the ear canal – something that can have unpleasant consequences. Always take care when using ear cleaners like this.

If you want to show your British Shorthair, you may need to give it a bath. Always do this a few days before the date of the show so that the coat has time to settle down. According to the breed standard, British Shorthairs should have small ears, so most exhibitors carefully pluck out the hairs that grow beyond the edges of the ears or trim them off. Cut the sharp points off the claws with good nail clippers.

Physical characteristics

BODY

The British Shorthair differs from an ordinary domestic cat not only in the quality of its coat but also, and primarily, in its build, which is not dissimilar to that of the Persian. British Shorthairs are medium-sized to large cats. They should have a deep chest, broad shoulders and a short, muscular back. The legs are short and straight, with strong, round paws. The thick tail is short to medium in length, with a rounded tip.

HEAD

The British Shorthair has a round, massive head, with full jowls and a broad skull, set on a short, thick, muscular neck. The small ears are short, broad at the base and set wide apart. The eyes are large and round; the color

Silver-tipped British Shorthair

Blue British Shorthair

varies, depending on the coat color. The broad nose is short and straight and the nose break should not be too pronounced.

There should be a gentle curve from the nose into the round forehead. The chin is strong and well-developed. An evident stop is regarded as a fault on the show bench. Adult males have a larger, more massive head than females and have the typical tomcat jowls.

COAT
The dense, short coat should feel slightly crisp and resilient. Because of its thickness and density it does not lie flat, but stands out very slightly from the body. Some British Shorthairs have coats that are too woolly, too long or too soft. These cats are not suitable for showing.

COLORS
British Shorthairs' coats come in a great many different colors, patterns and markings. The best known and still the most popular color, however, is self blue. A Blue British Shorthair is sometimes erroneously identified as a Chartreux.

Self colors
The self-colored British Shorthair occurs in a wide range of colors, including white, black, blue, red, cream, chocolate and lilac.

Self-colored British Shorthairs should have eye colors ranging from copper to orange, with the exception of the White, which may

have two blue eyes or be odd-eyed. With the exception of the White, there may be no white hairs or markings in the coats of self-colored British Shorthairs; every hair should be the same color from the tip to the root. This is known as 'solid to the roots.'

Some self-colored kittens have traces of tabby markings in the coat. This is known as 'ghost marking.' Sometimes these faint tabby markings remain visible in the coat when the animal gets older. These ghost markings are considered a fault on the show bench, although judges are sometimes prepared to turn a blind eye to them in the case of Cream and Red British Shorthairs because it is extremely difficult to breed a truly solid-color coat in these shades. A self-colored cat with a silver-white undercoat is known as Smoke.

Particolors
Particolors are colored cats with white areas in the coat. There are various versions, each with its own name depending on the amount

Black Smoke British Shorthair

Young Blue and White Bi-color British Shorthair

Black and White Bi-color British Shorthair

Blue and White Bi-color British Shorthair

Black Tortie and White Tri-color British Shorthair

of white in the coat and the type of markings. The best-known are the Bi-color and the Tri-color. In both cases, the white areas should cover no more than one-third of the total body area but not much less.

The Bi-color always has a self-colored coat and the white areas do not cover more than a third of the body. For show purposes, the markings should be as symmetrical as possible and an inverted white V on the forehead is always a plus.

The same rules apply to Tri-colors, but instead of a single basic color they have two basic colors (one of which is always red or cream), forming large, regular patches that do not blur into one another. If the main color of a Tri-color is black, it is also sometimes referred to as Black Tortie and White, and if the main color is blue, the color can be called Blue Tortie and White or Blue-Cream and White. Tortie and White is known as Calico in the United States.

It is difficult to breed a good particolor British Shorthair because mating two well-marked particolored animals is no guarantee that the kittens will turn out the same. Particolors with a lot of white in the coat are known as Harlequin and Van. The Harlequin has one or more colored spots on the head, a few small spots on the body and a colored tail. The Van only has color on the head and a colored tail. Aside from the fact that they are extremely attractive in their own right, crossing a Van or a Harlequin with a self-colored cat will often produce correctly marked Bi-colors or Tri-colors. The latest colors and patterns in the particolored group are Chocolate and White, and Tabby and White.

Black Tortie British Shorthair kitten

Blue Tortie British Shorthair

Tortoiseshell or Tortie

Cats that have different colored patches in their coats, but no white markings, are known as Tortoiseshells or Torties.

These cats are almost always female. Unlike the Tortie and White cats, which have clearly defined areas of color, the patches in these cats should be small and evenly intermingled, creating a very striking marbled effect. Main colors include black, blue, chocolate and lilac, while the other color is always red or cream. The eye color must be copper to orange.

Tabbies

There are four different tabby patterns– ticked, mackerel, spotted and classic. Tabbies are usually found in black, red, or blue, although other colors are possible. The tabby markings should be as clearly defined as possible. Tabbies with a silver undercoat are very popular. The eye color should be copper

to orange, except in the case of the Silver Tabby, which is bred with orange or green eyes.

Silver

These attractive varieties of British Shorthairs have not been around for all that long, but

Red Silver Classic Tabby British Shorthair

Blue Silver Classic Tabby British Shorthair

they are already very much in fashion. The silver undercoat is caused by a gene known as an inhibitor, which inhibits the formation of pigment at the base of the hair, in other words from the root. This means that each individual hair is partially without pigment at the root end – to the human eye this appears

silver. The rest of the hair has normal pigmentation and can therefore be black, red or another color. A distinction is drawn between self-colored cats and tabbies with a silver undercoat.

Black-shaded Silver British Shorthair kitten

When the inhibitor gene is present in a self-colored cat, this is known as Smoke. At shows, judges like to see the pigment covering about half of each individual hair. In the case of tabbies, various names are used, depending on the amount of pigment in the coat and the color of the pigment. In a Shaded Chinchilla, approximately one-third of each individual hair contains pigment, and in a Tipped Chinchilla the proportion is about one-eighth. These names are only used for cats with black pigment or colors derived from it, such as blue, chocolate and lilac. If the pigment is red or cream, the cat is known as a Cameo.

The pigment covers about one-third of the coat. Cats with coats this color where an eighth of the hair has pigmentation (in other words the tip of the hair only) are described as Shell and Chinchilla. If one-fourth of the

Chocolate Silver Tabby Point British Shorthair

Blue Point British Shorthair kitten

hair length is colored at the tip, the coat is called all shaded; if one-half of the hair length is colored at the tip, it is called all smoke. The amount of pigment in the coat can vary from one kitten to another in a litter, so it is up to the breeders to select cats with the desired pigmentation.

A tabby cat whose coat is half pigmented is not referred to as a Smoke because this name is reserved for self-colored cats; instead it is known as a Silver Tabby.

Some Chinchilla and Shaded Silver cats that are not purebred for the inhibitor factor can produce what are known as Golden offspring. These are actually Black Tabby cats

Chocolate Point British Shorthair kitten

whose pattern, as in the case of the Silver Tabby, has been bred out by selection.

Colorpoints

The latest – extremely attractive – coat color developed in the British Shorthair is the colorpoint. To achieve this, a few British and Dutch breeders have crossed Colorpoint Persians with British Shorthairs. Colorpoints come in all of the colors found in the Colorpoint Persian Longhair and, just as with the Persians, the contrast between the color of the body and the colored points (also sometimes referred to as the Himalayan factor) must be as distinct as possible.

At the moment, most Colorpoint British Shorthairs still have light blue eyes, but breeders are working towards cats with a dark blue eye color.

Special points

Because Persians are occasionally crossed into British Shorthair blood lines, a mating of two British Shorthairs can sometimes result in a surprise in the shape of one or more long-haired kittens (see Chapter 9, Semi-longhair Varieties, British Semi-longhair).

European Shorthair

There has been a great deal of confusion surrounding the name European Short-hair in recent decades because until 1982 there were two different short-haired breeds, both known as the European Shorthair and with the same breed standard. These were the European Short-hair bred on the Continent – a breed with Persian blood in it, known as the British Shorthair since 1982 – and the breed developed in Scandinavia from short-

haired farm cats without the influence of the Persian Longhair. The Scandinavian European Shorthair is the only cat now allowed to be called by this name, and the breed now has its own breed standard. The European Shorthair is not one of the thirty-six breeds registered by the CFA,

Red European Shorthair

the largest association of breed organizations in the United States.

European Shorthairs look like the ordinary domestic cats we see every day in Europe and the United States. The coat colors may only be the 'natural' colors, which means that these cats are only bred in black, red, blue and cream – with or without white markings or tabby patterns in the coat – and all white. Colors like chocolate and lilac, and the Himalayan factor found in the Siamese, are not permitted in this breed. Because the European Shorthair tends to look rather 'ordinary' among the many other, more exotic breeds of cat, the breed is not particularly popular. European Shorthairs are bred almost exclusively in Scandinavia, where they are frequently seen at shows.

The European Shorthair has been developed from sturdily built domestic cats like this one.

Temperament

Because the breed has been developed from ordinary domestic cats, which have very different temperaments, the character of the European Shorthair is impossible to sum up in a nutshell. Members of this breed may be very affectionate and will happily spend hours curled up on your lap, but there are others that prefer to be out mousing. To a certain extent, temperament is inherited. It is therefore wise to look at the characters of the sire and the dam before buying a kitten. Most European Shorthairs are strong and healthy, and as a rule they are friendly.

They get on very well with other cats and tolerate dogs well. European Shorthairs are intelligent and playful, and most of them are expert at keeping your house and garden free of mice.

Care

A European Shorthair's coat requires little in the way of grooming. It is usually enough to brush the cat once a week with a pig-bristle brush and to comb it with a medium-fine comb. When the cat is shedding, a rubber brush or massage mitt can be very useful in getting loose, dead hairs out of the coat.

The disadvantage is that you can damage the coat if you do not use these aids properly. Only clean the ears if they actually need it. Use a special ear cleaner for cats, which you can get from any good pet shop.

Cut the sharp points off the claws with good nail clippers every now and then.

Physical characteristics

BODY
In terms of temperament and appearance, the sturdy European Shorthair is comparable to ordinary domestic European short-haired cats. The conformation and the whole look of the cat reinforce this impression. The

European Shorthair is a muscular, medium-sized to large cat, with a broad, well-muscled chest. The strong legs are average length and the paws are round. The tail is fairly thick at the base, tapering to a rounded point.

HEAD
The relatively large head is rounded, with well-developed jowls, but it is certainly not as round as a British Shorthair's head.

The ears are medium-sized, and are as long as they are broad at the base, with a slightly rounded tip. They are quite wide-set and upright. The eyes are round and may be of any color that complements the coat color.

COAT
The European Shorthair's dense coat is short, soft and glossy. It should lie flat. A coat that stands out is a fault.

COLORS
All natural colors are permitted, such as black, red, blue and cream, with or without tabby or white markings. Pure white is also permitted. The eye color corresponds to the coat color and may be yellow, green or orange. Blue or odd-eyed individuals are permitted if the coat color is white.

Black Tortie American Shorthair

Bob Schwartz

American Shorthair

In terms of temperament and appearance, the American Shorthair is the equivalent of the European Shorthair. This breed is very popular in the United States, but these cats are seldom found anywhere else.

History

Excavations and other research have enabled archaeologists and scientists to establish that there was no indigenous cat population in North America before the fifteenth century. It is generally assumed that the first short-haired, more or less domesticated cats were taken to America by explorers and settlers from Europe.

It was standard practice to take cats on long sea voyages, because they made themselves

Red Silver Classic Tabby American Shorthair

Bob Schwartz

59

very useful keeping down the vermin on board ship. Once ashore they could continue their work on the farms. In due course they spread throughout the continent of North America, wherever the colonists settled.

The American Shorthair has developed from these hardy animals. It is a pedigree cat bred and selected with a view to the natural beauty of a street cat that many people regard as ordinary, without any crossbreeding with other non-indigenous breeds.

Temperament

The character of the American Shorthair is similar to that of the European Shorthair, which means that temperament can vary from one individual to another. What these cats do have in common, however, is that they are playful and remain so until a fairly advanced age, and most of them need space.

If you are not in a position to let an American Shorthair out of the house, it is highly advisable to invest in a large scratching post.

American Shorthairs are generally healthy and intelligent animals that get on well with other cats and pets. Generally speaking these cats are healthy and will live to a ripe old age.

Care

An American Shorthair's coat is easy to look after. When the cat is not shedding, brush the coat about once a week with a pig-bristle brush and then polish it with a chamois to bring out the shine. When the cat is shedding, a rubber brush or massage mitt can be very useful in getting loose, dead hairs out of the coat.
The disadvantage is that you can damage the coat if you do not use these aids properly.

As with all breeds of cat, cut the sharp points off the American Shorthair's claws regularly with good nail clippers and keep the ears clean.

Physical characteristics

BODY
The American Shorthair has a medium-sized to large, strongly-built body that is slightly longer than it is tall.

The chest is deep and broad, and the shoulders are well developed. The muscular legs are average length with heavy bones and large, powerful, round paws.

The tail is average length, broad at the base, and tapers to a blunt tip.

HEAD
The American Shorthair has a round head with full cheeks, slightly longer than it is wide.

The nose is average length with a slight break and the muzzle is square. The strong chin is well developed and forms a straight line with the upper lip when viewed in profile. The ears are medium-sized, spaced well apart and have a rounded tip. The wide-set round eyes have an alert and clear expression.

COAT
The glossy coat is short and thick. It may feel harsh or soft depending on the coat color and the time of the year. The coat can be considerably thicker and heavier in the winter than it is in summer.

COLORS
Because this cat is a natural farm or street cat breed and the influence of non-indigenous cats is not valued, the breed is bred only in natural colors, such as black, red, blue and cream, with or without tabby or white markings, and with a silver undercoat. Pure white is also permitted.

Colors like chocolate, Burmese markings and points are not allowed.

The eye color depends on the color of the coat, but is usually copper or green. White cats may be blue-eyed or odd-eyed.

Chartreux

The Chartreux is a blue, short-haired cat of a sturdy type. The breed is sometimes confused with the Blue British Shorthair, and in terms of type they are similar. The main physical differences are the shape of the head and the shape, position and size of the ears. In the past Chartreux were occasionally mated with Blue British Shorthairs, but breeders have decided that this is undesirable and it is no longer allowed.

History

There are a great many hypotheses about the origins of the Chartreux's name, but none of these has ever been proved beyond doubt. There are, however, records of blue-coated cats in both Rome and France as early as the sixteenth century, and in the eighteenth century the name 'Chartreux' cropped up regularly in books to refer to blue, short-haired cats from Paris.

From the sound of it, these cats may well have come from an isolated, mountainous region of France known as Grande Chartreuse. The Carthusian order of monks had a monastery here as early as the eleventh century, and it is said that blue cats had been kept by the monks for as long as people could remember. This hypothesis is far from unlikely. In the past people only kept animals that were of use.

Cattle, pigs, sheep and goats were kept for milk, hides, wool and meat. Cats were popular because they helped keep the thriving vermin population within bounds. When someone moved and settled elsewhere, he took not only his food and wool supply with him in the form of his livestock, but also at least one cat. The monks would certainly have been no exception. Since the region in question was difficult to get to, the cats that the monks took with them would have been unable to mate with cats from elsewhere, so that over the years a population of closely related cats of very similar appearance and characteristics grew up. To this very day there

has never been any conclusive evidence that this is indeed what happened, and the origin of the name Chartreux remains a matter for conjecture.

The breed is still very popular in France and Belgium and there are often large Chartreux classes at French and Belgian shows. Elsewhere, however, there is relatively little interest in the breed.

Temperament

Broadly speaking, the temperament of the Chartreux is similar to that of the British Shorthair.

The Chartreux is a friendly, good-natured cat with an equable, placid temperament. It gets on well with other cats and with dogs. Members of this breed make excellent companions for children because they seldom if ever show their claws if something upsets them – instead they simply remove themselves to a more peaceful spot. There is no need to be home all day if you have a

Chartreux as a pet, but it is not fair to the cat to leave it alone for most of the time. Consider getting two animals if you have to be out a lot. Chartreux love to play and climb, but they are not as conspicuously active as some of the other short-haired breeds. Their rarely heard voices are soft and unobtrusive.

Care

The Chartreux needs relatively little grooming. Brushing the double coat is a no-no, which means you will want to stroke the cat frequently, running your fingers through the fur and finishing with a chamois.

If the coat is very dirty you can use an unscented grooming powder, which absorbs dirt and excess grease. Leave the powder to work in for a few minutes and then stroke the cat until every trace of powder has been removed.

Clean the outer ear area with an ear cleaner specially designed for cats. If you want to show your Chartreux, clip the sharp points off the claws with a good pair of clippers beforehand.

Physical characteristics

BODY
The Chartreux is a medium-sized to large, muscular and sturdily built cat, and the toms, in particular, are very solid-looking animals. Chartreux have fairly long legs and large paws.

The medium-length tail is broad at the base, tapering to a rounded tip. When laid along the back the tail should reach to the hollow between the shoulder blades.

HEAD
The Chartreux's head is an inverted trapezium, slightly longer than it is broad. The nose is straight, broad and long, without a stop.

The ears are of medium size and set high on

Chartreux

the head, which gives the cat an alert expression. The eyes are large; they should not be too round, and the outer corners of the eyes should curve up slightly. Adult males have definite jowls.

COAT
The Chartreux has a double, glossy coat with a slightly woolly undercoat. The coat should not lie flat; it ought to stand away from the body slightly and feel soft to the touch.

COLORS
Every shade of blue from ash to slate-gray is permitted, but cats with an ash-gray coat are the most popular.

The coat tends to be more silvery on the nose, the whisker pads, the back of the ears and the tips of the paws.

The eye color is a golden copper to amber. There must be no hint of green in the eyes, which may fade as the cat gets older.

Special points

Most kittens have a very slight tabby pattern in the coat – ghost markings – at birth, but this disappears as they grow up.
A Chartreux is fully grown by the age of about two and a half.

Exotic

The Exotic is the short-haired variant of the Persian. This means that the breed standards are virtually identical, with the exception of the coat. This breed is a good choice for people who like cats of the Persian type but are not prepared to put in the significant amount of time that is essential in caring for a Persian's coat. All of the colors found in the Persian occur in the Exotic and these breeds are frequently crossed.

Blue Exotic

History

The first Exotic was produced in the United States relatively recently. A breeder who kept both American Shorthairs and Persians mated an American Shorthair tom with a Persian Longhair dam, producing a litter of

Harlequin Black Tortie Exotic

Red and White Exotic

kittens that were unmistakably Persian in type, but had inherited their father's short coat. Word of these kittens soon got around and they were generally thought to be so attractive that it was decided to set up a breeding program to establish the short-haired coat in the Persian type.

Burmese, as well as Persians and American Shorthairs, were used initially, but it is now general practice to cross Exotics and Persians only, because they are essentially the same breed with the same breed standard, except for the length of the coat. The aim was and still is, after all, to breed a short-haired Persian.

Because Exotics are still cross-bred with Persians, most litters contain some long-haired and some short-haired individuals.

Black Tortie Exotic

Blue Tortie with White Tri-color Exotic

The kittens are registered either as Exotics or as Persian Longhairs, depending on the length of the coat.

Temperament

Exotics are placid, docile cats with an equable temperament. Generally speaking their character is the same as a Persian's.

They have a soft, pleasant voice that they rarely use. Exotics usually get on well with other cats and have no problems with dogs, either. They are very good with children. Exotics are extremely adaptable and are perfectly happy in a lively household. If things get a bit too exciting they will find a quiet place somewhere in the house.

This breed tends not to be obtrusive. As a rule they go their own way, although they appreciate your company and love to be cuddled.

Care

An Exotic's coat can be kept in good condition with the minimum of grooming. Generally speaking you can brush the coat once a week with a soft pig-bristle brush and then comb it through with a coarse comb. Go about this gently to avoid damaging the coat. When the cat is shedding heavily you can use a rubber brush, which quickly and easily

Red Exotic

Persian Longhair and Exotic, two kittens from the same litter.

removes all of the loose hair. Be careful, however, since it is all too easy to pull out healthy new hair growth if you overdo it.

For shows, you can rub bran or an unscented grooming powder into an Exotic's coat. This should be brushed out of the coat again almost immediately. Bran and powder attract dirt and excess grease, so that the coat will look clean and fresh again after one of these beauty treatments.

Experienced exhibitors regularly pluck the dead hair out of the coat by hand, but this job requires a certain degree of knowledge and skill.

An Exotic's tear ducts may sometimes become blocked. It is therefore important to keep the hair around the eyes, the corners of the eyes and the creases in the face as clean as possible. Special lotions have been developed for the purpose. These are available at the better pet shops, and can certainly be purchased at most cat shows. The lotion should be applied with a soft tissue and then

carefully patted or wiped off again with a dry tissue. Because the breed standard calls for small ears, most exhibitors will carefully pluck out or trim off any hair growing along the edge of the ear, since this makes the ears look larger.

Use a special ear cleaner to keep the ears clean and trim off the sharp points of the claws regularly using good clippers.

Black-shaded Silver Point Exotic kitten

Black Tortie Exotic

Physical characteristics

BODY
The standard for the Exotic is the same as for the Persian Longhair except for the coat. The Exotic is a medium-large to large cat with a strong bone structure.

The body is compact, with a deep chest, muscular shoulders, a muscular back and a short, powerful neck. The legs are short and sturdy, and the paws are large and round. The tail is short, in good proportion to the body, and has a slightly rounded tip.

HEAD
The head is round, massive and well-proportioned, with a broad skull and full cheeks. The forehead is nicely rounded and the short, very wide nose has a noticeable break. The top of the nose should be in line with the lower eyelid. The stop should be level with the middle of the eye. The Exotic has strong, wide jaws and a firm chin. The teeth should have scissor-like action. Viewed in profile, the chin, the top of the nose and the forehead should be in a straight vertical line.

The small ears are wide at the base and rounded, with full ear furnishings. They are set wide apart and low on the skull. The large, round eyes are wide-spaced and should be bright and very expressive. The eye color is copper or dark orange, green or blue, depending on the coat color. Odd-eyed Exotics are also permitted. The color should be as pure as possible.

COAT
The coat of the Exotic, which is also sometimes referred to as the Exotic Shorthair, is soft and dense; it should never lie flat but must always stand out from the body slightly. The hair is slightly longer than a British Shorthair's.

COLORS
Because the Exotic is a short-haired Persian, the breed comes in all of the colors recognized for the Persian Longhair.

Self colors
Self-colored Exotics can be white, black, blue, red, cream, chocolate and lilac. Exotics with these coat colors have orange eyes – the darker the better – although White Exotics may also have blue eyes or odd eyes. The self-colored Exotics may not have any white

Black Classic Tabby Exotic, profile

markings and preferably no white hairs in their coats. Each individual hair should be the same color from the root to the tip, but in practice the hair is usually slightly lighter at the root.

Kittens often have ghost markings, and in some cases this faint tabby patterning remains visible when they become adults. Although judges dislike these markings in adult animals, ghost markings in Cream and Red Exotics will not be judged too harshly since it is extremely difficult to breed these colors without a trace of tabby. Self-colored Exotics with a silver undercoat are called Smoke.

Particolors
Particolors are colored cats with white areas in the coat. There are various versions, each with its own name depending on the amount of white in the coat and the type of markings.

Vans are Exotics that are predominantly white with two spots of color on the head and a colored tail. Harlequins are very similar to Vans but they also have one or more colored spots on the body.

The Bi-color always has a self-colored coat and the white areas do not cover more than a third of the body. For show purposes, the markings should be as symmetrical as possible and an inverted white V on the forehead is always a plus.

The same rules apply to Tri-colors, but instead of a single basic color plus white they have two basic colors forming large, regular patches that do not blur into one another. If the main color of a Tri-color is black, it is

Black Chinchilla Exotic

also sometimes referred to as Black Tortie and White, and if the main color is blue, the color can be called Blue Tortie and White or Blue-Cream and White. Particolors always have orange eyes.

Black Classic Tabby Exotic

Torties
Tortoiseshell or Tortie Cats that have different colored patches in their coats, but no white markings, are known as Tortoiseshells or Torties.

Unlike the Tortie and White cats, which have large, clearly defined areas of color, the patches in Tortie cats should be small and evenly intermingled, with no white, creating a marbled effect. The main color of a Tortie is always black or a derivative of it, such as blue, chocolate and lilac. When the main color is black, the other color is always red. When the main color is blue, chocolate or lilac, the other color is cream. Tortoiseshell cats with a silver undercoat are called Smoke.

Tabbies
There are four different tabby patterns: ticked, mackerel, spotted and classic. Tabbies may be black, red, cream, blue, chocolate or lilac. The tabby markings should be as clearly defined as possible.

A spotted tabby, for example, should have separate dark tabby spots that are as round as possible and do not run into one another. Tabbies with a silver undercoat are discussed under the heading Silver. With the exception of the Black, Chocolate, Blue and Lilac Silver Tabbies, Tabby Exotics should have orange eyes. There are also Tortie Tabbies; these cats have both tortoiseshell and tabby makings and are almost always female.

Colorpoints
In the Colorpoint Exotic, the contrast between the color of the body and the colored points must be as distinct as possible. Colorpoints are bred in all of the colors found in the Colorpoint Persian Longhair.
Colorpoint Exotic breeders and fanciers aim to achieve a very dark blue eye color.

Silver
Exotics with a silver undercoat include (Black) Silver Tabbies, Cameos, Chinchillas and Smokes. The silver undercoat is caused by a gene known as an inhibitor, which inhibits the formation of pigment at the base of the hair, so only part of each individual hair is pigmented – to the human eye it appears as if the undercoat is silver, but in fact there is simply no pigment there. A distinction is made between non-agouti cats (including the self-colored cats and the torties) and the agoutis, or tabby cats. When the inhibitor gene is present in a self-colored cat, this is known as Smoke. Judges at shows like to see approximately half of each hair with pigment. In the case of agouti or tabby cats the name varies depending on the amount of pigment in the coat and the color of the pigment.

In a Shaded Chinchilla, approximately one-third of each individual hair contains black, blue, chocolate or lilac pigment, but if only the very end of the hair is pigmented, the color is known as Tipped Chinchilla. If the pigment is red or cream and covers a third of the hair, the cat is known as a Cameo.

Cats with coats this color where an eighth of the hair has pigmentation (in other words the tip of the hair only) are described as Shell. In these cats the tabby marking is no longer distinguishable, because the color lies like a haze over the silver.

A tabby cat whose coat is half pigmented is known as a Silver Tabby. In these cats the tabby markings are still clearly visible.

Black-shaded Silver Point Exotic

Manx

The Manx is a centuries-old breed that developed naturally and is still kept by the farmers of the Isle of Man as a mouser and a cherished pet. Members of this breed are striking and yet at the same time unremarkable cats.

Unremarkable in that their common farm cat appearance does not impress people who like cats with a more exotic look, but striking because their tails are usually extremely short, consist of only a rise (known as a 'rumpy riser'), or are non-existent (a 'rumpy').

There is a general misconception that Manx cats have difficulty jumping and climbing; in fact the absence of a tail does not appear to hamper the cat's mobility in any way.

Manxes are healthy animals with a friendly, affectionate and intelligent temperament, making them excellent pets.

History

This breed has its origins on the Isle of Man, in the Irish Sea off Britain's west coast. In all probability, a spontaneous mutation occurred there around four centuries ago, resulting in the birth of a tailless kitten.

This animal survived to become a strong adult and was able to reproduce, so that gradually more and more tailless cats were born on the island. The isolation of the island allowed the tailless strain to predominate and eventually there were more cats without a tail than with one.

The existence of these unusual cats did not escape the attention of cat fanciers in other parts of the world. There are reports of imports as early as 1830, and Manxes were appearing at shows in the United States and on the Continent by about 1890. Today, interested breeders and fanciers still visit the Isle of Man to look for suitable breeding animals.

The tremendous interest shown by cat lovers from off the island led the Manx government to establish an official cattery in the 1950s, in order to call a halt to the outflow of cats.

Rumpy Manx

At that time, anyone who was interested in a Manx could approach this stud. The cattery was privatized in the early nineties. It ran at a loss and was eventually closed down. Now the tourist office in the capital, Douglas, refers enquiries to private breeders. The breed still has official protected status on the Isle of Man.

Rumpy Manx

In the rest of the world, the tailless cat is regarded as a curiosity, but on the Isle of Man they think that cats with tails are unusual.

A well-known European Manx breeder once had a conversation with an old farmer who asked her whether it was really true that mousers like his were regarded as very special pedigree cats. The breeder nodded. Then the farmer asked her whether cats elsewhere were kept the same way he kept his – roaming around the farm in complete freedom. Again she nodded. Finally, the farmer asked whether it was true that these cats all had tails. The breeder could only nod again. The farmer looked off into the distance for a moment and then said, "That must look really funny, all those cats with tails." This story illustrates just how established tailless cats are on the Isle of Man.

Temperament

Manxes are placid cats. Generally speaking, they are affectionate cats that get on well with other cats and with dogs, as well as with adults and children – although they do have a tendency to become particularly attached to one member of the family.

You can teach a Manx to fetch balls of wadded-up paper and train it to walk on a lead. Despite their placid and equable natures, Manxes are extremely playful and remain so until they are quite old. You should make sure that they have plenty of toys and a

Rumpy riser Manx

Manxes are friendly cats.

sturdy scratching post. Although they lack the tail that people assume a cat needs to 'steer with', they are extremely accomplished climbers and hunters (how else could they have survived all these centuries without catching mice and other vermin?).

Manxes are relatively healthy cats that can live to an advanced age if they are well looked after.

Evidence of their vitality is provided by a Manx queen, being kept in the Netherlands, who became world champion at the 1996 world championship show at the age of ten and a half.

The average show age for a cat is between one and three years old, and this queen is the only cat in the world to have achieved a triumph of this kind at such an advanced age.

Care

A Manx's coat does not require a great deal of grooming. It is enough to brush the coat once a week with a soft pig-bristle brush and then comb it through gently with a coarse comb. When the cat is shedding you can use a rubber brush, which quickly and easily removes all of the loose hair.

Be careful, however, since it is easy to damage the coat. As with all cats, you should check a Manx's ears regularly and trim the sharp tips off the claws from time to time.

Rumpy Manx

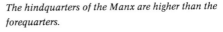

The hindquarters of the Manx are higher than the forequarters.

Physical characteristics

BODY

The Manx is a sturdy, medium-sized cat with good bone structure. It has a round, compact build. The hind legs are clearly longer than the front legs, so that the back slopes upwards. The legs are muscular.

There are five different tail lengths. The completely tailless Manx is known as a Rumpy; the Riser (or Rumpy riser) is a cat with no more than three coccygeal vertebrae (equivalent to the vestigial 'tail' or coccyx in humans) and no tail vertebrae; the Stumpy has a short stump tail; the Longie is a cat with a normal-looking but abnormally short tail; and the Tailed is a Manx cat with a full-length tail.

The first three more or less tailless varieties can be shown; the last two are used in breeding provided they are good in terms of type.

HEAD

The head is round, with a sloping nose line. The ears are not set too high, they are broad and open at the base and they turn slightly outward. The eyes are large and round.

COAT

There are two recognized Manx varieties, the shorthair and the semi-longhair (see Chapter 9, Semi-longhair varieties, Cymric). The short-haired Manx has a double coat that feels very soft and thick, because the soft, short undercoat pushes up the medium-long topcoat.

COLORS

Manxes are only bred in natural 'farm cat' colors, in other words the colors found in ordinary European domestic cats. 'Non-natural' colors include chocolate and 'Burmese coloration'; colorpoints and ticked tabbies are likewise not considered as 'natural' coat patterns. These colors and patterns are consequently not found in this breed. Common Manx colors are red, black and blue, possibly in a tabby pattern and with white markings, and pure white. The eye color is of less importance in the Manx: yellow, green and shades of yellow-green all occur, but white cats may also be blue-eyed or odd-eyed (with one blue and one yellow eye).

'Golfsticks,' a Black Manx from around the turn of the century.

American Bobtail

The American Bobtail is a breed that is seldom found outside the United States, its country of origin. The breed is the result of a mutation that occurred in a few domestic American cats. The fact that this cat has a short tail does not affect its mobility in any way, and American Bobtails can climb and hunt with the best of them.

As a rule, American Bobtails are very attached to their human family, but they can be rather shy with strangers. They are happy in the company of other cats and get on well with dogs. Most American Bobtails enjoy being around people and do not like being left alone for any length of time.

American Bobtail

Bob Schwartz

half-length tail with a number of kinks. A definite bobtail that is not too long is required for show purposes.

Physical characteristics

This is a medium-large to large breed and it may be two or three years before an individual is fully grown. For showing, judges like to see cats with a straight tail reaching halfway to the hock, although the tail may be slightly curved.

The American Bobtail has a muscular body set on medium-length legs; the hind legs are always longer than the front legs. The paws are round and large. The weather-resistant double coat may be semi-long or short, and both varieties of this breed are easy to care for. (See also Chapter 9, Semi-long-haired varieties, American Bobtail, semi-longhair.) However, this is not a breed that is recognized by the CFA.

Special points

The way in which the bobtail is inherited has not yet been established. It is known that it is caused by a dominant gene, which means that cross-breeding with suitable domestic cats can produce kittens with a short tail. The length and shape of the tail is pretty variable – from virtually absent altogether to an almost

Japanese Bobtail

Old writings and drawings show cats with deformed tails existed in China more than a thousand years ago. It seems clear that the Chinese cats are the ancestors of the Japanese Bobtail. Although the Japanese have kept short-haired domestic cats with short bobtails or even kinked tails for centuries, a long time passed before they were discovered by cat fanciers elsewhere.

The first Japanese Bobtails seen outside Japan were taken to the United States in 1968, and the breed is now popular mainly among American and Japanese cat-lovers.

These exceptionally attractive and intelligent cats are virtually unknown in the rest of the world and are seldom seen at shows. The breed is, however, registered by the CFA.

Japanese Bobtails have a decidedly active, extroverted and lively temperament. Because they are so curious, very little escapes these cats and their intelligence means that you can teach them tricks, such as retrieving a wad of paper. The breed gets on very well with other cats and with dogs.

Short-haired Japanese Bobtail

Long-haired Japanese Bobtail

Bob Schwartz

Physical characteristics

Japanese Bobtails take their name from their short, tightly-curled tails, which range from 5 to 8 centimeters (up to 4 inches) long and may be straight, curved or kinked. The body and legs are muscular, long and lean, and the paws are oval. The wedge-shaped head has high cheekbones and the eyes are large and oval. The large ears are upright and should be set neither too high nor too low, but approximately at the 'corners' of the triangular face. The coat lies flat against the body and there is virtually no undercoat. The fur is soft and silky. One striking feature of the Japanese Bobtail is that it sheds very little.

There is a shorthair and a semi-longhair Japan-

ese Bobtail (see Chapter 9, Semi-long-haired varieties, Semi-longhair Japanese Bobtail).

All coat colors are permitted, but the most popular cats are those that are predominantly white with a few black and red, clearly visible, deep colored markings in a calico pattern, known to the Japanese as 'mi-ke' (pronounced mee-kay and meaning three-fur). This coat color is regarded as lucky by the Japanese. All eye colors are permitted in the Japanese Bobtail and odd-eyed forms are also found.

Scottish Fold

A cat that always manages to attract the attention of the general public at shows, the Scottish Fold is striking because of its folded ears and round skull, which give the cat a quirky and sometimes rather melancholy look. Fans of the breed think it looks like an owl. Scottish Folds are friendly and good-tempered.

History

In 1961, a white cat with folded ears appeared in a litter of kittens born to a farm cat in Perthshire, Scotland. The kitten, a tom, was named Snowball and soon attracted the interest of breeders. With the aid of suitable domestic cats and British Shorthairs, the particular mutation responsible for the folded ears was established in a new breed under the

Blue Classic Tabby Scottish Fold

Black Mackerel Tabby Scottish Fold

name Scottish Fold. The factor that causes the cat's folded ears is inherited as a dominant trait.

Sadly, it initially appeared that this gene not only caused the characteristic folded ears but may also have resulted in abnormal cartilage elsewhere in the body, particularly if both parents had folded ears. This was one of the reasons why the British association temporarily withdrew the provisional status as a

breed that had been granted to the Scottish Fold. Careful breeding since that time, however, has created a hearty, healthy breed. Meanwhile, Folds have been exported to the United States, and the breed is also bred there.

Because the gene can lead to skeletal abnormalities in homozygous (purebred) form; two cats with folded ears are never mated together. Instead, Folds are bred to cats with normal ears from Fold bloodlines (Scottish Straights), American Shorthairs or British Shorthairs. Cats imported from the United States and their descendants are now also to be found in some European countries.

Temperament

The Scottish Fold is a friendly cat with a docile nature. They are generally placid, although they are by no means averse to play.

They get on well with other cats and they seldom have problems with dogs provided that they are introduced to them in a positive way as young kittens.

Scottish Folds are not easily upset and are perfectly at home in lively families. They make excellent playmates for children. If a Scottish Fold is treated too roughly, its initial response will be to remove itself from the situation.

It is only likely to use its claws as a very last resort. Scottish Folds are by no means vocal

Scottish Fold

Scottish Fold kitten

Black and White Scottish Fold

Blue Scottish Fold

and seldom use their quiet voices. Although they like to be picked up and cuddled, they will not pester you for attention.

They like company, but most Scottish Folds can stay on their own for a day without becoming concerned.
They make ideal pets for people who want a placid cat and like the amusing look of these Scots.

Care

A Scottish Fold's coat can be kept in good condition with the minimum of grooming. When the cat is shedding, you can use a rubber massage mitt to remove loose, dead hair from the coat. You should brush the coat with a bristle brush or comb it with a comb that is not too fine in order to avoid damaging the undercoat.

Because the Scottish Fold's ears are folded forwards, many people assume that they are more prone to ear infections, but this is not the case. The ears require no more attention than those of other cats and can simply be cleaned with a special ear cleaner for cats every now and then. Trim the sharp points off the claws occasionally.

Physical characteristics

BODY
The Scottish Fold is a medium-sized, muscular cat with a fairly heavy bone structure. The rump is rounded and the legs are short to medium-length in relation to the body. The paws are round and attractive. The tail is medium-length to long. A long tail, tapering to a point, is preferred. At a show, a Scottish Fold will be disqualified if irregularities (kinks) are found in the tail, if the tail is shorter than usual or if it is not flexible enough because the vertebrae are abnormally thick. Cats that show any other skeletal abnormality will also be disqualified.

HEAD
The round head is carried on a relatively short neck. The jaw is well-developed, much more so in males than in females. The eyes are large and round, and fairly widely spaced with a friendly, good-tempered expression. The nose is very short with a slight stop. The ears are folded forward and downward. Cats with small, tightly-folded ears will be more successful at shows than animals with larger, looser ears. The Scottish Fold's ears should lie against the head like a cap, emphasizing the roundness of the skull. The tips of the ears are rounded.

A litter of Scottish Folds can contain kittens with folded ears and kittens with normal ears Scottish Fold.

COAT
The Scottish Fold's double coat is very dense and feels soft and resilient. It is important for the coat to stand out from the body; a coat that lies flat will lose points at a show.

COLORS
The Scottish Fold can be bred in any coat color, provided it is 'natural.' The Himalayan factor found in Siamese is not permitted in the Scottish Fold, nor are colors like chocolate, cinnamon or lilac.

The most common colors are blue, red, black and cream, sometimes with white and a tabby marking, and pure white is also recognized.

The eye color corresponds with the coat color, but is usually copper or orange.

Special points

For health reasons, Scottish Folds are never normally mated with each other.

In Europe they are generally crossed with British Shorthairs and in the United States with American Shorthairs. The kittens that result from these crosses all have upright ears for the first few weeks of their lives. The ears of the kittens that carry the gene for folded ears start to fold over when the kittens are three or four weeks old.

Scottish Fold

The others retain their upright ears and are known as Scottish Straights. There is also a semi-longhair Scottish Fold, known as the Highland Fold (see Chapter 9, Semi-long-haired varieties, Highland Fold).

American Curl

The American Curl with its backward-curling ears is a very distinctive cat. This breed came about relatively recently and American Curls are still a rarity outside of the United States. These cats are seen in a short-haired and semi-longhair form. All colors are recognized.

History

In June 1981 Joe and Grace Ruga found a half-starved black female cat with strange ears in Lakewood, California. They adopted the kitten, which they called Shulamith (meaning black and homely), and she became the founder of the American Curl breed. Shulamith thrived and in December of the same year she gave birth to four kittens. Two of them had curled-back ears just like their mother. Curious about the genetic background to this phenomenon, Grace Ruga got in touch with a geneticist who came to the conclusion that this was a spontaneous mutation and that the gene causing the curly ears was a single dominant gene.

Fanciers found the curled-back ears so charming and attractive that they decided to set up a breeding program to establish this mutation. The breed was officially admitted to the Championship Class in the United States in February of 1993.

Temperament

The first thing you notice about an American Curl is its affinity with people. American Curls are inquisitive and intelligent, and like to be involved in everything that goes on in the household.

They love to be petted and adore being the center of attention.

They are equable animals, not easily put out, and this makes them ideal for lively families with young children, for whom they make splendid playmates. However, the children must not be allowed to pull the cat's ears or try to bend them forwards. Obviously no one should do this to any cat, but it is particularly painful for the American Curl. Members of this breed remain playful and adventurous all their lives. You would be well advised to buy a sturdy climbing post on which your pet can work off its energy, and stock up on plenty of toys.

American Curls are not particularly vocal, but they have their own ways of telling you what they want: they will sit and stare at you unblinkingly or constantly get under your feet. They get on extremely well with other cats and live very happily with dogs as well.

Red-shaded Silver American Curl

bob Schwartz

Care

Because they have virtually no undercoat, it is very easy to keep these cats in good condition. You need do no more than brush the coat about once a week and then comb it with a fine comb.

Trim the claws regularly and only clean the ears when necessary, using an ear cleaner specially designed for cats.

You can bathe this cat from time to time, but always use a proper cat shampoo.

If you plan to take your American Curl to a show, it is a good idea to bathe the cat a few days before the show so that the coat has time to settle down.

Physical characteristics

BODY
The American Curl is a medium-sized cat with a long, lean, elegant body.

All parts of the body must be in proportion and the cat should be neither too stocky nor too slender. It can take two or three years for an American Curl to grow to full maturity.

HEAD
The head is slightly wedge-shaped and should be longer than it is wide. The ears are the American Curl's most distinctive feature; they feel less flexible than those of other breeds. They stand upright at the corners of the head and curl smoothly backwards with the tips pointing towards the center of the base of the skull.

An American Curl has a straight nose, a strong chin and large, walnut-shaped eyes.

COAT
An American Curl's coat may be short or semi-long; there is virtually no undercoat. The coat should feel soft and silky. There must always be ear furnishings curling outward from the inside of the ear, and small lynx tufts on the tips of the ears are considered to be a plus.

COLORS
This breed is bred in every conceivable color and pattern. The reason for this is that the original cat was crossed with domestic cats that had numerous inherited color factors. Breeders consequently decided to aim for as much variation as possible.

Special points

Because the gene that causes the American Curl's ears to curl back is not linked to any adverse side-effects, the cats can be mated with one another and with (non-pedigree) domestic cats which, with the exception of the ears, are as close as possible in type to the American Curl breed standard. Because the gene is inherited as a dominant trait, most of the kittens produced by these crosses will have backward-curling ears, even though they carry the gene for normal ears and can pass it on to subsequent generations. An American Curl with normal ears is known as an American Curl Straight Ear. When they are born there is no visible difference between kittens with straight ears and kittens with the curl – the ears do not take on their definitive shape until the kitten is about four months old. (See also Chapter 9, Semi-long-haired varieties, American Curl, semi-long-hair).

Munchkin

Munchkin

The Munchkin is a fairly recent develop-ment originating from a cat with mutated, extremely short legs. The existence of this new breed of cat caused a furor in the United States. In France, where the first Munchkin exported from the United States was taken, the breed has also created a stir in cat fancy circles.

History

In 1983, in the state of Louisiana, two cats with extremely short legs were found in the street. One of them proved to be pregnant and subsequently gave birth to four kittens. Two of them also displayed this peculiarity. A number of breeders picked up on this and the variety was developed through crosses with

Munchkin

suitable domestic cats. The Munchkin, as the breed had since been dubbed, was recognized by one of the cat associations in the United States in 1995.

Munchkins are currently bred in the United States and in France, where a number of individuals were taken.

Temperament

Munchkins are lively, playful cats. The Munchkin can play and climb trees like any other cat, but its short legs prevent it from jumping as high as cats with normal legs.

A Munchkin will not be able to get up on the kitchen counter or the table without an intermediate stop on the way. Munchkins are sociable pets that get on extremely well with other cats and dogs.

They are very affectionate and like to be part of whatever is going on.

Care

The short-haired Munchkin needs little in the way of grooming. All you need to do is brush the coat once a week, and follow up with a fine comb.

Clip the claws regularly and clean the ears, but only when necessary, with a special ear cleaner for cats.

Physical characteristics

BODY

The Munchkin is a medium-sized cat with a broad, deep chest and a medium-length tail that tapers slightly to a rounded tip. The straight, muscular legs are very short and the hind legs are longer than the front legs.

Cats with turned-in hocks and cats with an excessively stocky or excessively elongated body will not do well at shows. Paws that turn in or turn out, a clear dip in the back behind the shoulders and bent legs are considered faults and Munchkins with any of these characteristics will not qualify for shows.

HEAD

The Munchkin has a medium-sized, slightly wedge-shaped head with large, upright ears. The large, expressive eyes are walnut-shaped and slightly slanting.

COAT AND COLORS

A Munchkin can have a short or semi-long coat. (See also Chapter 9, Semi-long-haired varieties, Munchkin, semi-longhair).

Special points

Because the gene that causes this breed's short legs is dominant, a cross between a Munchkin and a normal cat will produce Munchkin kittens in the first generation.

For the time being only crosses with ordinary short-haired and long-haired domestic cats that are not of any other pedigree breed are permitted.

Russian Blue

The Russian Blue is a delightful breed with an elegant appearance, an unusual coat color and texture, and bright green eyes. Russian Blues like a quiet life and become very attached to the people around them.

History

As the name suggests, it is assumed that the Russian Blue comes from Russia. But the origins of this breed, like so many others, cannot be established with certainty.

Russian Blue

It appears that around two hundred years ago there were cats with blue coats in the area around Archangel, a port on the White Sea. English merchants brought these blue cats back to Britain in the mid-nineteenth century, and they were widely exhibited under the name 'Russian Shorthair', 'Maltese Blue' or 'Archangel Blue.'

Nowadays it is standard practice to show each breed separately, but at the end of the nineteenth century it was customary to show all blue-haired cats in the same class. This fact almost brought about the downfall of the Russian Blue, because the judges tended to prefer other short-haired blue breeds, particularly the British breeds.

The Russian Blue suffered in consequence and, if not for the fact that separate classes were set up for foreign breeds in 1912, the breed would probably have died out. The Russian Revolution meant that the British

Russian Blue

Russian Blue

public had a very low opinion of anything that was even remotely Russian, so from this period until 1939 the breed was shown under the name 'Blue Foreign'. The Second World War brought another threat to the Russian Blue.

There were few true to type individuals left by the end of the war, so in order to prevent too much in-breeding the breeders were compelled to introduce foreign blood. The breed they chose for the purpose was the Blue Point Siamese, which certainly contributed to the re-establishment of the breed but at the same time meant that the Russian Blue started to become finer and finer in type and increasingly like a Blue Oriental Shorthair, with a coat that was too smooth and flat.

In the mid-sixties a group of breeders decided to get together and try to breed back the traditional, distinctive Russian type. Happily, they have succeeded.

Today's Russian Blue is again a unique breed in terms of both character and appearance, and the resemblance to the Orientals has significantly diminished.

The basis was laid in the United Kingdom, but magnificent Russian Blues were and are also bred in Sweden and the United States. The breed has now spread all over the world from these three countries.

Since the fall of the Iron Curtain, authentic bloodlines from Russia and former East Bloc countries have become available.

Russian Blue

Temperament

The influence of the Siamese in keeping the Russian Blue going as a breed would lead you to suspect that the Russian has inherited a great many character traits from its Oriental relatives, but nothing could be further from the truth. The temperament of the Russian Blue is unlike that of any other cat. Although they can sometimes be very playful and will remain so until they are quite old, they are essentially quiet by nature.

Russian Blues like their comforts and will happily spend hours lying in the same place, preferably on a lap belonging to a member of the family. Most Russian Blues hate noise and fuss, and they can find life exceedingly trying in a house with small children. Russian Blues are very shy with people they do not know. They will usually disappear if there are visitors and they do not appreciate being stroked or picked up by strangers. They are highly unlikely to lash out with their claws – they are far too gentle for that – but they will certainly let it be known that they do not like it. Members of this breed generally get on well with other cats and dogs. They have very pleasant, quiet voices; even dams in heat seldom make much noise.

Care

The Russian Blue's distinctive coat requires relatively little care. All you need do is brush the coat occasionally with a soft brush. Too much combing or the use of a rubber brush when the cat is not shedding can damage the soft undercoat and even drag it out of the skin. Clean the ears with an ear cleaner when necessary. Trim the sharp points off the claws regularly using good clippers.

Physical characteristics

BODY
The body is relatively long. It should be neither too stocky nor too lean. The impression should be one of grace and elegance. The long legs show relatively fine bones and the paws are small and oval. The Russian Blue has a long, tapering tail that may not be too broad at the base.

HEAD
The head is broad, moderately wedge-shaped and may not be too long. The ears are set high on the head; they are broad at the base and reasonably large, tapering to a point.

There is virtually no hair on the inside of the ear. The nose profile should be as straight as possible, running into the flat skull without a stop. The almond eyes are wide-set and may not be too small. The chin is strong and the whisker pads should be prominent. The neck is long and powerful.

COAT
The Russian Blue's double coat is short, silky and fine-textured. It has an exceptionally soft feel. The coat should never be too flat or close-lying, but should stand out

slightly from the skin to emphasize the plush texture. The texture of this cat's coat is unlike that of any other breed.

A long-haired version of the Russian Blue was bred fairly recently: it is a separate breed which has been named Nebelung. (See Chapter 9, Semi-long-haired varieties, Nebelung).

COLORS

Russians are bred in three different coat colors. Blue-gray is the oldest, best-known and most popular color, but a growing number of cats of this breed are being born with black or white coats, although they are not yet recognized by all of the associations. The blue coat should be blue-gray and as even and pure in color as possible, with a soft, silvery sheen. Ghost markings or white hairs in the coat will be marked as faults on the show bench. The nose and paw leather is also blue-gray and the eyes should be an intense green. Yellow tints in the green are regarded as a fault, but it may take some years for the eventual vivid green color to develop.

The Russian White is pure white, with a pink nose and pink pads; the eyes are green, odd-eyed (one green and one blue eye) or blue. The Russian Black is pure black, with dark nose and paw leather. This color also has the distinctive green eyes.

Korat

The Korat is a slender, short-haired cat with an Oriental conformation and a blue coat. Breeders of the Korat want to keep the breed as pure as possible, and it is consequently strictly forbidden to cross a Korat with another breed. The Korat is rare and even in its native country, Thailand, there are very few of them.

Korat

History

The Korat is named after the province of Cao Nguyen Khorat, where the breed originated. In Thailand, the cat is known as 'Si-Sawat', the bringer of good fortune. Centuries ago, in the Cat Book Poems written in Thailand (then Siam) sometime in the late Middle Ages, the Korat is described as having "smooth hairs with tips like clouds and roots like silver, and eyes that shine like dewdrops on a lotus leaf."

The first Korats to leave Thailand were taken to the United States around the end of the nineteenth century. Nowadays the breed is found all over the world, although it remains rare, even in its country of origin.

Temperament

Korats are extremely affectionate cats with a very distinct character. They become very attached to the people around them and need a lot of love and attention.

Generally speaking they get on well with other cats, although some Korats may become jealous if members of the family pay attention to other pets. The breed is extremely intelligent: you can easily teach them to retrieve and they will quickly learn to walk on a lead.

Korats have a very melodious voice and are highly vocal. They are lively, active and playful, and they love to climb.

Care

The Korat's short coat can be kept in good condition with the minimum of effort. It is generally enough to brush the cat's coat with a pig-bristle brush about once a week. When the cat is shedding you can use a rubber brush, which quickly and easily removes all of the loose hair.
Clip the claws regularly, using good clippers, and clean the ears if necessary with a special ear cleaner.

Physical characteristics

BODY
The Korat has a semi-Oriental body, which means that it should be lithe and lean, but not as slender as a Siamese.

The front legs of this attractive cat are shorter than the hind legs and the back is slightly curved. The cat is strong and muscular, which means it is actually heavier than it looks. The tail is medium-length and broad at the base, tapering to a rounded tip.

HEAD
The Korat has a heart-shaped head with large, high-set ears. The length of the nose is in proportion to the size of the skull and it has a slight break. The eyes are large, and oversized in relation to the face. They look quite round when the cat opens them wide, but the shape is unmistakably Oriental.

COAT
The Korat's glossy, short-haired coat feels like satin; there is no undercoat, so the hair lies flat against the skin.

COLORS
The correct shade of blue is highly rated at shows. The hair is lighter at the roots, darkening along its length; the tip of each hair has a silvery sheen, creating a very unusual effect.

At shows, Korats with clear green eyes are likely to do well, but young animals may also have amber eyes because it can take anywhere from two to four years for the eye color to develop fully. Lilac Korats have also been bred recently.
The chocolate factor responsible for this coat color came with the cats from Thailand, where many cats exhibit it.

Siamese

Even people who know virtually nothing about cat breeds will be able to recognize the Siamese with its characteristic coat pattern, mysterious blue eyes and long, svelte body. The Siamese has been a popular pedigree cat for a very long time, yet a Siamese is not the best choice for everyone. Siamese cats are very extroverted and not everyone can live with a cat that is as demanding as this one. However, if you are looking for a pedigree cat with a lively and very affectionate nature that requires little in the way of grooming, a Siamese might be the ideal breed for you.

History

The origins of the Siamese lie in the Far East. No one knows exactly where the first Siamese

Seal Point Siamese

Seal Point Siamese

Blue Point Siamese

came from, but these animals were known in Thailand, formerly Siam, as early as the fourteenth century. They became known to the rest of the world through the royal family of Siam: what better gift to present to a visiting dignitary than these beautiful native treasures? British travellers in Thailand also noticed the breed at the end of the nineteenth century. The British were only familiar with ordinary house or farm cats and Angoras, which were very much in fashion at the time, and they had never before seen anything like these cats with their long bodies, distinctive markings and short, soft coats. They took a number of Siamese home with them, and their wives fell head over heels in love with these animals. They did everything possible to make the cats feel as much at home as possible. Most of them kept their cats in heated conservatories with tropical plants that their husbands had brought back from previous voyages.

Meanwhile, the French had also discovered the elegant Siamese and these exotic cats were frequently seen at the earliest cat shows.

The Siamese of that period were very different in conformation from the Siamese of today. The earliest Siamese were considerably more sturdily built and their heads were fairly round, rather than triangular. A breed characteristic that was regarded at that time as highly desirable and evidence of pure breeding was a pronounced squint and a kink in the tail. It is interesting to note that the

Blue Point Siamese

Cream Point Siamese

Siamese kept in the temples of Siam did not display these abnormalities!

The first imports from Thailand were Seal Points, but later these cats spontaneously produced kittens in other colors: Blue Point, Chocolate Point and Lilac Point. These four colors, all solid, are the 'classic' Siamese colors, and all of the colors produced since are the result of cross-breeding. This is why Siamese in colors other than the four classic colors are not recognized in the United States. (Tabby and Tortie Points, Red, Cream

Cream Point Siamese

and Cinnamon Points are classified as a separate breed under the name Colorpoint Shorthair.) These non-classic colors were developed in the United Kingdom. In the 1950s and 60s British breeders started to breed Siamese in other colors, using Russian Blues, British Shorthairs and others. The influence of these breeds produced the Tabby Points, Red Points, Cream Points and Tortie Points, and not so long ago more new colors were introduced, including Cinnamon and Fawn Point. Now there are also Siamese with a silver undercoat on the colored points: the Silver Tabby Point and the Smoke Point. The most recent additions are the Bi- and Tri-colorpoint Siamese.

Temperament

Anyone planning to buy a Siamese should be aware that these cats have a very strong character and always make their presence in

Chocolate Point Siamese

Blue Tabby Point Siamese

stroked and petted and will spend hours sitting on your lap. They are ideal pets for people who want company: these animals can gauge their owner's mood perfectly, and are almost always lively and amusing. Siamese are playful cats that love all sorts of toys in the shape of ping pong balls, wadded-up paper or fur mice. Most Siamese will quickly learn to retrieve paper or balls, and usually take quite readily to walking on a lead. When you get a Siamese, you are not just getting a cat: you are getting a real personality. Siamese will return the love and attention they receive with interest.

Care

The short coat, with its silky texture and little or no undercoat, tends not to get dirty, so Siamese require virtually no grooming. While

Siamese kitten

the house felt. These animals are often referred to as the dogs of the cat world – and with good reason. Siamese are known for their vociferous nature and they can keep up a conversation with you – or with themselves – for hours on end. They may be hungry, they may want attention or there may be something that meets with their disapproval, but whatever the reason they will let you know about it at the top of their raucous voices. Siamese queens in heat are notorious in this respect and their calls can be heard halfway down the block. Siamese are extremely sociable creatures and if they are not getting enough attention they will demand it. Because they like company so much they cannot be left alone for too long. If you are out at work all day, you would be wise to get more than one cat or even consider not getting a Siamese at all.

Siamese get on very well with other cats and exceptionally well with dogs. They like to be the center of attention. They love to be they are shedding you can remove loose, dead hairs quickly and easily with a damp chamois and then, if necessary, comb through with a fine comb.

If you want to show your Siamese, you may want to bathe your pet to make it look especially good. Always use a shampoo specially formulated for cats, and bathe the cat a few days before the show so that the coat has time to settle down again.

Siamese have sharp claws and you should clip the tips every now and then with good clippers. Clean the ears – but only when necessary – with an ear cleaner made specifically for cats.

Siamese love company (Chocolate Tortie and Cinnamon Point).

Chocolate Tortie Point Siamese

Physical characteristics

BODY
The Siamese, like the Oriental Shorthair, is a breed with an elegant, lithe conformation. The svelte body is long, lean and muscular; there may be no sign of coarseness. The hind legs, like those of the wild members of the cat family, should be longer than the front legs. The legs are long and slim, and the paws should be oval. The tail is long and thin, tapering to a point, like a whip. A kink in the tail is a fault.

HEAD
The head is wedge-shaped. Ideally, the face and the large, diagonally-set ears should form a perfect equilateral triangle. The chin should not be too pronounced, but it definitely may not recede. At shows, judges will check to see that there is a level bite.

Siamese have almond-shaped eyes that should be a deep, dark blue and slightly slanted. They should not be too deep-set. Siamese cats have long noses, preferably with a Roman profile, but in any event running straight to the top of the head without a stop.

COAT
A Siamese's coat should be silky to the touch and very short and fine-textured. Siamese have relatively little undercoat. Overlong hair, excessive undercoat or a coarse texture are all regarded as faults.

Siamese are very vocal.

A Siamese from around the turn of the century.

Chocolate Tabby Point Siamese

COLORS

Siamese kittens are all white when they are born, and their colored points – on the face (or mask), ears, tail and legs – do not appear until later.

By the time a Siamese is about three years old the coat will have developed its permanent color. The light-colored areas of the coat may become slightly darker over the years as a result of a cold ambient temperature and the licking of the coat.

The hair can also get darker at places where the skin has been damaged. Siamese that seldom if ever go outside or live in a warm climate are generally purer in color. At shows, cats that have too may dark shadows in the coat will lose marks.

Breeding light-colored coats is extremely difficult, particularly in the Seal Point and the Blue Point, because this shadowing on the body is extremely common in these colors

and is very difficult to breed out. Another problem is encountered in breeding pure colored Red Points and Cream Points. The undesirable tabby markings – which appear as rings on the animal's tail and as barring on the mask and legs – are almost always present in this color, making Red and Cream Siamese with solid points almost impossible to tell

Siamese kittens from around the turn of the century –
note the white paws of the kitten on the right.

Mrs. Roberts Locke with her cats Calif, Siam and Bangkok.

Foreign White

Although most white cats with blue eyes are deaf or, if mated together, have a very great chance of producing deaf kittens, this is not the case with the Foreign White. This is because under their white coats they are actually Siamese. Siamese are always born white and their darker points do not show up until later, but the Foreign White stays as white as it was the day it was born. The Foreign White's blue eye color consequently comes from the (pointed) Siamese and not from the gene that is responsible for blue eyes – and also causes the related deafness – in other white cats.

In terms of temperament, the Foreign White is just like the Siamese. Both are social, vociferous animals, extremely attached to people, affectionate and intelligent. The Foreign White's coat does not require special care. When the cat is

Foreign White

apart from Red and Cream Tabby Points. The original Siamese colors are Seal, Blue, Chocolate and Lilac Point, but Red and Cream Points are also very popular. Seal, Blue, Chocolate and Lilac Points also occur in Tortie and Tortie Tabby forms. These cats are almost always female. More recent colors include Cinnamon, Fawn, Smoke, Silver Tabby and Bi- and Tri-color Point.

Foreign White

Special points

There are breeders who have remained faithful to the 'old' type of Siamese. Because they do not conform to the present breed standard, they are bred under other breed names.

In the United States they are sometimes referred to as 'Apple Head', and the term Thai is also used to denote a Siamese of the old type.

93

shedding, use a damp chamois to remove loose, dead hair from the soft, silky coat which has very little undercoat, finishing off with a fine comb. If you want to show your Foreign White, it may sometimes be necessary to bathe your cat a few days before the show. Always use a shampoo specially formulated for cats, and never bathe the cat the day before a show because the coat needs a few days to settle down again.

Physical characteristics

The Foreign White is a white Siamese, so the breed standard is exactly the same with the exception of the coat color. This must be pure white, with no hint of yellow or any other color. Foreign Whites may not have any dark pigment: the pads on the feet, the inside of the ears and the nose are therefore always pink. The eyes are always blue. At shows, judges will be looking for Foreign Whites with the deepest and liveliest dark blue eye color.

Oriental Shorthair

The Oriental Shorthair (also known in the United Kingdom as the Foreign Shorthair) is similar to the Siamese in terms of type and character. The difference between the two breeds lies primarily in the coat color and the color of the eyes. The colored

Blue Oriental Shorthair

Chocolate Oriental Shorthair kitten

points seen in the Siamese are absent from the Oriental Shorthair. Oriental Shorthair cats also have emerald-green eyes instead of blue. In recent years these cats have been bred in many different colors and color combinations, and breeders are currently working on more new colors that will undoubtedly be seen in the future.

History

The Oriental Shorthair is the result of crosses between Siamese, non-pedigree cats and other breeds. Around 1950 several breeders – most of them British – decided to try to breed a Siamese without the characteristic Siamese points.

To achieve this, they crossed Siamese with ordinary domestic cats and with other breeds, such as Abyssinians. The very first Oriental Shorthairs were Havanas, but a great many colors have since appeared. Although the breed has not been in existence all that long, there are breeders and aficionados of these cats all over the world.

Oriental Shorthair kitten

Temperament

The character of the Oriental Shorthair is broadly comparable to the Siamese. Some people say that the Oriental Shorthair is not as noisy, but this is not necessarily so. Like the Siamese, Oriental Shorthairs generally get on extremely well with other cats, and can become very good friends with dogs. They are good with children.

Oriental Shorthairs are sociable animals, so if you are out a lot it is wise to get more than one cat so that they can keep each other company. The worst thing you can do to an Oriental Shorthair is to leave it alone at home or in an outside run all day. It may simply pine away, but it is more likely that a lonely

Blue Classic Tabby Oriental Shorthair kitten

animal like this will express its protest by demolishing your furniture and by spraying.

Oriental Shorthairs are affectionate and like to be stroked and cuddled; they will become insistent if you do not give them enough attention.

They are very playful and remain so until they reach an advanced age. Ping pong balls, wadded-up paper and fur mice all make suitable toys. Because they are very intelligent cats with a sociable nature, it is relatively easy to teach them tricks. Most of them will enjoy retrieving scraps of paper and they will generally take readily to walking on a lead. It dos not matter if things sometimes get a bit rough at playtime; Oriental Shorthairs can take the occasional knock and enjoy a good rough and tumble. Oriental Shorthairs like to be the center of attention and will usually subject your visitors to a thorough inspection and demand to be stroked. Oriental Shorthairs are inquisitive and very little escapes their notice.

White Bi-color Oriental Shorthair

a damp chamois to remove loose, dead hair from the coat, but do this with care.

If you want to show your Oriental Shorthair you may want to bathe it. Always do this a few days before the show, with a shampoo specially formulated for cats, to give the coat time to recover. Trim the sharp claws regularly with good clippers and keep the ears clean with a special ear cleaner, which you can get from your vet, from good pet shops and at cat shows.

Physical characteristics

BODY

The Oriental Shorthair is a medium-sized cat with a slender build and fine bones. The cat must have a lithe, svelte and elegant appearance and may show no trace of coarseness anywhere. The hind legs are longer than the front legs and the legs themselves are long, slim and fine-boned. The paws are oval. The tail is long and thin, tapering to a point.

The combination of curiosity and intelligence can sometimes give rise to problems because it will take them no time at all to work out how to open a particular door, and enterprising individuals will soon fathom the mysteries of taps and kitchen cupboards. Oriental Shorthairs are ideal cats for people who like an extroverted, affectionate and playful cat and are charmed by their elegant, lithe appearance. You can expect all the love you give them to be returned with interest.

Care

The Oriental Shorthair's coat needs relatively little care. The glossy, soft, fine coat does not get dirty quickly and it is usually enough to brush it through once a week with a soft brush. When the cat is shedding you can use

Oriental Shorthair kittens at five days old

Cinnamon Spotted Tabby Oriental Shorthair

Black Ticked Tabby Oriental Shorthair

Lilac Ticked Tabby Oriental Shorthair kittens

HEAD

The head is wedge-shaped and the face should form a perfect triangle with the large, diagonally-set ears. Strongly developed cheek muscles break up the line of the head and are therefore undesirable.

The chin should not be too pronounced, but it definitely may not recede, making the animal look as if it has no chin at all. The Oriental Shorthair's eyes are almond-shaped and slanting, with a lively, expressive look.

Chocolate Silver Ticked Tabby Oriental Shorthair

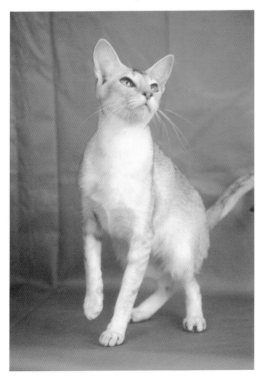

The nose is long and there is no nose break.

COAT

The Oriental Shorthair's coat should feel silky-soft. It is very short and fine. Oriental Shorthairs have relatively little undercoat. Overlong hair, excessive undercoat or a coarse texture are all regarded as faults.

Cinnamon Ticked Tabby Oriental Shorthair kitten

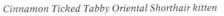

COLORS

Oriental Shorthairs should have green eyes – preferably dark green with no trace of any other color, such as yellow or brown. Oriental Shorthairs can be bred in innumerable colors and patterns with the exception of the Siamese (Himalayan) pattern. The most popular colors are Black (also known as Ebony) and Blue, but the Tabbies are also much in demand.

Self colors

The best known self colors in the Oriental Shorthair are Havana (Brown), Ebony (Black), Red, Cream, Cinnamon, Fawn, Lavender (also known as Lilac) and Blue. In the ideal animal, each individual hair is the same color from the root to the tip. There may be no tabby markings visible anywhere on the body, although kittens and young cats usually do have ghost markings.

In Red and Cream cats it is effectively impossible to get a completely solid coat color because the ghost markings always remain visible in these colors. When a self-colored cat has a silver undercoat, it is described as Smoke. There are also White Oriental Shorthairs. These are not the same as Foreign Whites. Unlike the Foreign Whites, White Oriental Shorthairs have green eyes or odd eyes.

Black Spotted Tabby Oriental Shorthair

Lilac Ticked Tabby Oriental Shorthair

Blι

Tabbies

There are four different tabby patterns: ticked, mackerel, spotted and classic. The Oriental Shorthair is bred in all of these patterns. With the exception of the ticked tabby, which has ticking all over the body, the tabby variants should have clear tabby markings in the coat. The tabby patterns should be as distinct as possible and give the impression that they have been painted on to the cat.

Well-defined rings that go right around the tail and dark necklaces that go all the way around the neck are regarded as very desirable.

There should be a clear, dark M (known as the scarab marking) over the eyes. Tabbies come in a range of colors, including black, blue, red, cinnamon and chocolate, with or without a silver undercoat.

Torties

Torties are usually female. The coat is patterned with small, irregularly-shaped spots of different colors, merging into one another. The basic color of a Tortie is black, blue,

Cinnamon Ticked Tabby Oriental Shorthair

Chocolate Silver Classic Tabby Oriental Shorthair

S

Tʰ
lo
wι
Aι
br

Tʰ
wι
m
a
bι
nι

H
—

Tʰ
Uː
cc
be
pɾ
Bι
m

T
—

Sι
bɾ
th
fa

Brown Burmese

latest additions to the color range are Cinnamon and Fawn.

Temperament

If you ask a Burmese lover what most attracts him or her to the breed, nine times out of ten the answer will be 'their personality.' The Burmese has an exceptionally sweet and loving nature. Burmese love company and are extremely inquisitive. These two qualities, added to the fact that most Burmese are fairly equable by nature, make them delightful companions who love to spend time with you.

Most Burmese will follow you around all day long and love to sit on your lap or lie on the paper you are trying to read. Contact with people is extremely important to these cats. The worst thing you can do to a Burmese is keep it in a separate room. People who are out a lot would do better not to get a Burmese.

Almost all Burmese are sociable. Queens are often happy to share the raising of a litter of kittens and Burmese seldom fight among themselves.

As a rule they get on well with dogs, and because they are so calm, laid-back and not easily upset, they make excellent playmates for children.

Burmese have quieter voices than Siamese and are perhaps not quite as vocal. Should you have gained the impression that the Burmese will spend the whole day curled up on the sofa with you, purring, this is only partly true.

While they do radiate an inner calm, what makes them so extraordinary is that they are also very active and playful – and remain so as they grow older.

Blue Burmese

Blue Burmese

Burmese love to play and never lose their appetite for fun even if they are neutered. They are also famed for their intelligence, and they can be quite self-willed and persistent when they choose.

Care

Because the Burmese has little or no undercoat, grooming will not require a lot of your time. If you stroke the cat regularly and brush the coat occasionally with a soft brush, it will retain its natural gloss and sheen.

Trim the claws regularly with good clippers and only clean the ears when necessary, using a special ear cleaner for cats.

Physical characteristics

BODY
The Burmese is a medium-sized cat. Queens weigh about 3.5 kilos (8 lbs) on average, but the toms are usually slightly larger and heavier.

The body is well-muscled and strong, with a straight back and a deep chest. The legs are slender in relation to the body, with oval paws.

The tapering tail is medium-length with a rounded tip. The Burmese's body and head should be neither too Oriental in type nor too stocky.

HEAD
The Burmese has a basically wedge-shaped head with rounded contours and a strong, broad lower jaw and chin. There is a distinct nose break.
The slightly forward-set ears are medium-sized, set wide apart and broad at the base, with a rounded tip. The eyes are large and also widely spaced. The lower lid is rounded and the upper lid is straight.

COAT
The Burmese has a very short, dense, close-lying coat with virtually no undercoat. The

Red Burmese kitten

Cinnamon Burmese kitten

texture of the hair is fine and satiny. A Burmese's coat has a wonderful deep shine.

COLORS
The Burmese coat color is truly striking, in shades not found in any other breed. The underparts are always lighter than the back

and the legs, and the colors shade subtly into one another. The cat's face and ears may contrast in terms of color, but marking, white hairs and barring in the coat are not allowed. Vague ghost markings are permitted in kittens up to the age of six months.

The color of the kittens is fairly light at birth, darkening as they get older. It may take a year or two for the coat to develop its final color and sheen.

There are many coat colors in the Burmese: Brown, Blue, Chocolate, Lilac, Red, Cream and Cinnamon. The silver factor has also been introduced recently.

Burmese are also bred in Brown, Blue, Chocolate and Lilac Tortie. Whatever the coat color may be, at shows judges are looking for golden-yellow eyes with no hint of blue or green, but this is a very difficult ideal to achieve in practice. The eye color can fade in older animals.

The shape and expression of the eyes are considered more important on the show bench than the color.

Special points

If you go to cat shows in the United States, the United Kingdom and mainland Europe, you will see different types of Burmese. This is because the breed standard in the United States calls for a more rounded, stockier type than the British standard, which is looking for a slimmer, slightly more Oriental type.

The most obvious difference is in the shape of the head. The American Burmese has an extremely short head with large, slightly bulging eyes. The head of the British Burmese is more moderate in shape. The type found in continental Europe is predominantly the British form. In recent years the

Cinnamon Burmese

Lilac Burmese

Cream Silver Burmese

Young Chocolate Tortie Burmese

Burmese has been used in the creation of a new breed, the Burmilla. This is a silver cat of Burmese type. The silver coloration comes from the Chinchilla Persian, and various colors and patterns are emerging from Burmilla crosses. Cats that are not silver ticked are known as Asian.

Bombay

The Bombay is a pure black cat with a 'patent leather' shine to its coat which in terms of conformation is most like a Burmese, although the head is somewhat more rounded. Sadly the Bombay is not widely bred, particularly in Europe, and the breed is relatively rare. Few breeders around the world have specialized in this beautiful breed.

History

American Burmese breeder Nikki Horner wanted to create a mini-panther. She started in 1953 by breeding a black American Shorthair to a sable Burmese. After years of selective breeding, she succeeded in producing a superb jet-black version of the breed. Bombays are now mated with one another and with Burmese.

Temperament

Generally speaking, the Bombay's character is similar to that of the Burmese. Bombays make excellent pets, getting on well with other cats and with dogs. They are very good with children.

Bombays are usually placid cats with an even-tempered, friendly nature. They need a lot of company and attention and do not take well to being left alone for long periods. Cats of this breed are seldom very vocal. They have a pleasant, quiet voice that is rarely heard.

Bombay

Care

The Bombay requires little grooming and is consequently easy to care for. The coat should be a deep jet black and very glossy. To achieve this effect, all you need to do is stroke the cat regularly and rub the coat with a chamois every now and then.

Physical characteristics

BODY
The Bombay's conformation is very similar to that of the Burmese, but the influence of the American Shorthair has meant that the Bombay is rather sturdier and has a more rounded head. The body is medium-size and muscular. The build should be neither too stocky nor too fine. The legs are moderately long, as is the tail, which should have no kinks or other irregularities.

HEAD
The head is rounded and broad. The muzzle should be fairly short and the nose should show a clear break at the transition to the forehead. The eyes are wide-spaced and round. The relatively small ears are set slightly forward. They are broad at the base and rounded.

COAT
The very short, close-lying coat should have a deep, patent-leather shine. The Bombay has virtually no undercoat. The coat should be the deepest possible jet black. There may be no white hairs or other markings in the coat.

Kittens may have a rusty-brown tinge to their coats, which disappears as they get older.

COLORS
This cat is usually black. Kittens of different colors may, however, be found in a litter of Bombays. Some will be black, others may have the typical Burmese color and color shading. The Burmese type kittens will not normally be used for breeding. Self-colored kittens (in other words without the Burmese factor) in chocolate, blue or lilac may also be born. These are not recognized. The most desirable eye color is copper, but golden-yellow eyes are permitted.

Tonkinese

The Tonkinese is a relatively rare breed and this is a shame, because this cat has a delightful character and beautiful looks - a combination likely to appeal to a great many people.

History

Oddly enough, the first known Tonkinese was Wong Mau, the founder of the modern Burmese line.

Wong Mau was found in Rangoon (Burma) in 1930 by the American Dr. Joseph C. Thompson, who was so charmed by her appearance that he took her back with him to San

Tonkinese with aquamarine eyes

Tonkinese with aquamarine eyes

Tonkinese have a positive attitude and are almost always good-tempered. They are good with children and get on well with other cats and with dogs.

If you have to be out a lot, you would be wise not to get a Tonkinese. Tonkinese want a great deal of love and attention and should not spend their days in a separate room or an outside run. They need to be part of the family. They are not as talkative as the Siamese, but will nonetheless be quite vocal.

Care

Francisco. People in the United States had never seen a cat with such an unusual brown coat, and thought that Wong Mau was a dark Siamese. It was subsequently proven that she was in fact a Tonkinese. Wong Mau was mated with a Siamese tom. The litter contained a brown tom, who was mated back to his mother. The kittens in this litter proved to be a lively assortment of cats with Siamese, Tonkinese and Burmese looks. All of the kittens with Tonkinese traits were eliminated from the breeding program, because the Americans were primarily concerned with producing kittens of the Burmese type.

In the 1980s, however, breeders in the United Kingdom started crossing Siamese with Burmese again in order to regain the attractive Tonkinese look.

The breed has now also been recognized in Britain and is popular in the United States.

Temperament

Tonkinese are ideal cats for people who want company. They are very attached to people and love being the center of attention. Because they are so inquisitive and intelligent you can teach them all sorts of things, including retrieving and walking on a lead, but these qualities also mean that a Tonkinese will have little difficulty opening doors and kitchen cabinets if it thinks there might be something interesting there.

The Tonkinese's short coat can be kept in good condition with the minimum of effort. It is generally enough to brush the cat's coat with a pig-bristle brush about once a week, following up with a chamois to bring out the shine.

Clip the claws occasionally, using good clippers, and clean the ears if necessary with a special ear cleaner for cats.

Physical characteristics

BODY
In terms of type, Tonkinese fall between the long, lean Siamese and the stockier Burmese. The cat should be muscular and is surprisingly heavy.

HEAD
The Tonkinese has a wedge-shaped head, with a blunt muzzle and prominent whisker pads with an indentation – known as the whisker break – behind them.

COAT
The coat is short and close-lying, and should feel soft and silky.

COLORS
The coat color of the Tonkinese is midway between Siamese and Burmese coloration. This means that the cat has clear points, but the body color is much darker than that of the Siamese. Tonkinese are bred in all of the

Bob Schwartz

colors and patterns that occur in the Siamese. In the United States all of the recognized Tonkinese colors are referred to as Mink.

The eye color is described as aquamarine. In fact it, too, is halfway between the blue eyes of the Siamese and the yellow eyes of the Burmese.

Special points

Kittens are light in color when they are born, but begin to darken up within a few days. This process continues: the older a Tonkinese gets, the darker its coat will become.

This variety can never be bred completely true, since it is an intermediate form between two albino genes which produce the Siamese and the Burmese colorations respectively. This means that a litter born to two Tonkinese may also contain Siamese and Burmese kittens as well as Tonkinese kittens.

Singapura

The Singapura is a breed that has been recognized relatively recently. It is still only bred on a small scale by a core of American enthusiasts.

History

The breed takes its name from the Malaysian name for Singapore. In 1975 Hal and Tommy Meadows, on a visit to Singapore, were captivated by the small, slimly built cats with an unusual coat color in a ticked tabby pattern that they saw roaming the streets of the city. They were so impressed that they decided to take a number of cats back to the United States with them in order to set up a breeding program and establish their exceptional features.

By the end of the 1980s the Singapura had been recognized by most cat associations, and since then the breed has been bred on a small scale by a hard core of fans. The breed is relatively unknown outside of the United States.

Singapuras can still be found on the streets and in the houses of Singapore, although they are likely to be in colors other than the warm dark brown ticked tabby pattern with a warm ivory background, which is the only color recognized in the West. The breed is only crossed within itself, which has kept it as pure as possible.

Temperament

Singapuras are friendly, affectionate animals and generally devoted to the people they live with. Some of them can, however, be shy in the presence of strangers.
Generally speaking, Singapuras are very inquisitive.

Cats of this healthy breed are usually fairly placid by nature, but they are also playful and remain so as they get older.

Care

The Singapura requires very little grooming. It is enough to comb the coat through once a week and polish it with a damp chamois to bring up the shine. Clip the sharp tips off the claws regularly and clean the ears, but only if necessary, with a special ear cleaner for cats.

Physical characteristics

BODY
The Singapura is a small to medium-sized cat with muscular legs and small, oval paws. The body is compact but may not be too stocky. The slender tail is medium-length to long and the tip of the tail is slightly rounded.

HEAD
The head is set on a fairly short, muscular neck. The lines of the head are rounded. The

ears are strikingly large. They are upright, and give the cat an alert expression. The large, almond-shaped eyes are green, outlined in dark brown. The nose pad is similarly outlined.

COAT
The Singapura has a short, soft, close-lying coat.

COLORS
The only recognized color for the Singapura is a seal brown ticked tabby with an ivory background, officially referred to as Sepia Agouti. Barring on the inside of the legs is permitted, but if the cat has stripes on the tail it will be disqualified at shows. A great deal of importance is attached to the correct coat color and the right ticking.

Singapura

Bob Schwartz

Abyssinian

Abyssinians are short-haired, elegant cats with a strong personality. They are probably one of the oldest breeds of domestic cat in the world. Some people believe that Abyssinians are the descendants of the cats of Ancient Egypt.

History

Many people believe that Abyssinians could be found at the Courts of the Pharaohs in Ancient Egypt. The similarity in appearance and conformation between the modern Abyssinian and mummified cats that have been discovered in excavations in Egypt is striking. The many illustrations and statues of cats dating from Ancient Egyptian times are said to bear numerous points of resemblance to today's Abyssinian. On the other hand, all of these finds, without exception, depict cats

Young Ruddy Abyssinian

Young Sorrel Abyssinian

Sorrel Abyssinian

with a slim, Oriental build, a wedge-shaped head and slanting, almond-shaped eyes, which could just as easily have been the predecessors of the Siamese or a local Egyptian cat that has since died out. There is no incontrovertible historical evidence either way.

What is certain, in any event, is that the first Abyssinian cat was brought from Ethiopia (Abyssinia) to Great Britain in 1868 by Field Marshal Sir Robert Napier. This cat, whose name was Zula, had the typical ticking in the coat, but otherwise bore little resemblance to our modern Abyssinians. It is believed that Zula is the founder of the Abyssinian line. Abyssinians were recognized in the United Kingdom in 1882 and appeared regularly, if in small numbers, at cat shows. The two world wars and a catastrophic outbreak of feline leukaemia almost wiped out the breed and it was not until the early sixties that the Abyssinian population started to recover. The breed is now one of the best known and most

Black Silver Abyssinian

One of the earliest Abyssinians with two Manx cats

popular short-haired breeds. The first Abyssinians to be imported to North America from England arrived at the beginning of the twentieth century, but it was not until the thirties that several top quality Abyssinians were exported from Britain to form the foundation of today's American breeding programs.

Temperament

Abyssinians are extroverted, wilful and intelligent cats. They are not very intrusive, but they do have their own particularly elegant way of letting their owners know exactly what they want. They do not use their quiet voices a great deal, because on the whole Abyssinians are not talkative. Abyssinians, or 'Abys' as they are affectionately referred to by

their fans, are real characters with very strong personalities. They need a great deal of contact with the family to keep them happy and will certainly pine away or protest if they are left to their own devices all day long. They like to be part of the family and want to be involved in everything that goes on. As a rule they get on reasonably well with other cats, and they can strike up lifelong friendships with dogs. Males are generally more easygoing than females, who can sometimes be a bit prickly with other cats. You are unlikely to find Abyssinians in crowded catteries because these are cats that need their space. Most breeders will consequently not have many Abyssinians, because they do demand a lot of attention. The worst thing you can do to an Abyssinian is to shut it up in a confined space.

Abyssinians are known for their intelligence and for their curiosity. Literally everything new that is brought into the house will be extensively investigated and inspected, whether it is a bag of groceries from the supermarket or a new piece of furniture. Despite this inquisitive streak, the average representative of the breed is not reckless. Abyssinians are sensible cats that do not take unnecessary risks.

They are also playful and adventurous. You can give them a sturdy scratching post and cat gym to play on, or perhaps an outdoor run with some tree trunks to climb. Once the cats have finished playing (and they will usually

This Abyssinian has a particularly attractive profile

113

An Abyssinian's 'boots'

Care

An Abyssinian's coat is fairly easy to keep in good condition. When the cat is shedding, you can use a rubber massage mitt to remove loose, dead hair from the coat. At other times, brush every now and then with a bristle brush, comb through with a fine comb and then polish with a damp chamois to bring out the shine.

It is good practice to trim the tips of the claws regularly. Check the ears every so often and clean them, if necessary, with an ear cleaner designed specifically for cats.

involve at least one member of the family in the game), they will happily lie on your lap for hours to be stroked and petted. But don't be fooled: in the Abyssinian Breeders International Kitten Buyer's Guide, Carolyn Osier calls the breed "...very good at training people to do just what they want them to do."

Physical characteristics

BODY

The Abyssinian's muscular, strong, lithe body is of medium length and moderately Oriental in type. It should not be too large or too coarse, and should certainly not be at all stocky. The legs are slender in proportion to the body, with a fine bone structure. The

Two young Ruddy Abyssinians

elegant paws are small and oval. The Abyssinian has a fairly long tail, broad at the base and tapering to a point.

HEAD

The head is broad and moderately wedge-shaped. There is a slight nose break and the chin is very definite. Ideally, the nose and chin form a straight vertical line when viewed in profile.

The almond-shaped eyes are slanting and have a lively expression. The relatively large ears are set low; they are broad at the base, tapering to a point. There are no furnishings inside the ear, but small tufts on the tips of the ears are a plus.

COAT

The Abyssinian's resilient coat is short, fine and close-lying. A coat that is coarse, too long or stands away from the body is considered to be a fault for showing purposes.

COLORS

The original Abyssinian coat color is known as Usual the United Kingdom and as Ruddy elsewhere, including in the United States. Over the years various other attractive colors have been developed from this original color, but the markings on the coat remain the same. The back of the hind legs and the pads of the paws, for example, are always darker than the rest of the coat irrespective of the color. All Abyssinians have striking ticking in their coat. On each individual hair the base color of the coat is interrupted by two or three bands of darker pigment, as found in the wild rabbit. The tip of the hair must always be dark.

The ticking should be as pure as possible and barring or spotting in the coat (particularly on the neck and legs) are considered undesirable on the show bench. All colors may have a little white on the chin and whisker pads, but it certainly should not extend too far. Abyssinians without a silver undercoat may sometimes have a grayish tinge to their coats. This is caused by gray roots in the hair.

This gray cast, like too much white, will lose marks at shows. Regardless of the coat color, the eyes are amber, green or yellow and should be as clear as possible.

Sorrel Abyssinian

Ruddy

Usual or Ruddy is the best-known and most common coat color. The coat has a warm reddish-brown base, with black ticking. In Ruddy Abyssinians, the feet and the backs of the hind legs (boots) are always black.

Sorrel

Sorrel is another popular color, albeit one that is not recognized by the CFA, the largest body of breed associations in the United States. As in the Ruddy, the coat has a warm reddish-brown base, but the ticking, the soles of the feet and the backs of the legs are cinnamon rather than black.

Blue

Blue Abyssinians have become increasingly popular in recent years. The base color of the cat is light beige, and the ticking, the pads of the paws and the 'boots' are steel blue. This is the dilute version of the Ruddy.

Fawn

Fawn Abyssinians are still relatively rare. The basic color of the coat is light cream, with darker cream ticking. The 'boots' and the pads of the paws are a warm dark cream. Fawn is a dilution of Red.

Silver

Silver Abyssinians are a separate group among the Abyssinians. Despite the fact that this color has been in existence for decades and is very attractive, it is another color that is not recognized by the CFA. In Silvers the undercoat is always a pure silvery white. The markings include black (Black Silver), blue

(Blue Silver), warm dark cream (Fawn Silver) and cinnamon (Sorrel Silver).

Good Silver Abyssinians are difficult to breed because they sometimes have undesirable tan patches in the coat. In addition to this, any barring in the coat shows up more clearly on a silver coat. A perfect Silver Abyssinian, however, is a really beautiful sight.

Tortoiseshell, Red and Cream

These rare colors are bred, although on a smaller scale, in Holland and the United Kingdom. It is not easy to achieve a good contrast in the Tortie pattern with a ticked coat.

The Red Abyssinians that have been produced, however, are a spectacularly bright color and the Creams are extremely elegant. Breeders in Holland and the United Kingdom are also breeding Chocolate and Lilac varieties. Red Abyssinian is a color recognized by the CFA in the United States.

Special points

Abyssinian kittens are born with dark coats that gradually lighten as they mature. It usually takes several months for the final coat color to become established. Because Abyssinians carry the gene for long hair it is possible to find Somalis in a litter of Abyssinians (see Chapter 9, Semi-longhaired varieties, Somali).

California Spangled

The most conspicuous characteristics of the California Spangled are their striking spotted tabby pattern and the extraordinary, springy and flowing gait that immediately evokes associations with the leopard. The cat's appearance would lead you to think that its ancestors were wild cats, but in fact only domestic cats were used in the breeding program.

History

The California Spangled is the creation of American Paul Casey. He had a specific aim in mind: to produce a new breed with a coat very reminiscent of a leopard's but with the temperament of a domestic house cat.

To achieve his goal, Casey used various pedigree and non-pedigree domestic cats in the breeding program. They included Abyssinians, Manx cats, Siamese, Persians, and American and British Shorthair, as well as ordinary domestic cats from the United States, and Asian street cats. No wild cats were involved. By continually selecting for animals with the right conformation, good musculature and, above all, the desired coat marking, Casey eventually succeeded in establishing the type he had had in mind years previously – the California Spangled, an extraordinarily successful breed in many respects.

The introduction of the California Spangled in 1986 was accompanied by a blaze of commercial publicity that provoked significant protest from cat lovers. In the Christmas edition of a famous department store's mail order catalogue, customers were invited to buy a California Spangled kitten for their sweetheart. For a huge sum of money, the customer could order a kitten – and the price included a beautiful gift box with ribbons and bows. There is a small group of breeders in the United States. The breed is not found elsewhere. It is not one of the thirty-six breeds recognized by the CFA, but there is a breed organization in California.

Temperament

California Spangleds are intelligent, active cats that love to play, run and climb. A good climbing frame and a scratching post are very worthwhile investments, and toys like fur mice, ping pong balls etc. will also keep these cats amused for hours. California Spangleds are generally sociable animals that get on well with other cats. They generally have few if any problems with dogs, either. Because they are so playful and tireless, they make ideal companions for children.

Care

The short-haired coat of the California Spangled is relatively easy to keep in good condition. It is generally enough to brush the cat's coat with a pig-bristle brush about once a week. When the cat is shedding, a special rubber brush is ideal for removing loose, dead hairs from the coat, but use it with care because you could inadvertently damage the coat if you are overly enthusiastic. If you want to take your cat to a show, you can bring up the gloss in the coat by polishing it with a damp chamois. Clip the claws regularly, using good clippers, and clean the ears if necessary with a special ear cleaner.

Physical characteristics

BODY
The California Spangled is a medium-sized cat with a long, lean, muscular body. A striking feature of the breed is the long, angular shape which ensures that the animal's movements are lithe and supple. The legs are long, but angled so that they appear shorter than they really are. The medium-length tail is

Gold California Spangled

Snow California Spangled

Bob Schwartz

the same thickness along its length, with a round tip.
Show faults include an overly long tail that tapers to a point, a stocky conformation, a body that is not well-muscled and a narrow chest.

HEAD
The head is medium-sized with broad, prominent cheekbones. The muzzle is full and well-developed, with a strong, firm chin. The ears have rounded tips and are set high on the head. The eyes are almond-shaped.

COAT
The California Spangled's coat is short, smooth and close-lying on the back and flanks, but rather longer on the underparts and tail. This breed is only bred in a spotted pattern, which should be clear and well-defined, with the greatest possible contrast. Barring or blotches in the coat are not permitted in this breed, and white markings and an overly long coat are serious faults.

The California Spangled is bred in several colors, including Black Silver, Charcoal (black spots on a sandy gray background), Bronze, Gold and Brown. The eyes are always amber to brown. If the spots are black, the eyes are sandy to yellow-gray. The Red and Blue spotted types should have gray-brown eyes.

The 'Snow Leopard' can have any of these coat colors; this variety clearly betrays the presence of Siamese influences. The Snow Leopard always has blue eyes. Green eyes are not permitted with any of the coat colors and are regarded as a fault at shows.

Egyptian Mau

The Egyptian Mau, say its devotees, is a direct descendant of the sacred cats of Ancient Egypt. It is the wonderful spotted patterning on the coat that makes this lively breed so striking.

History

Unlike that of all other domestic cats, the spotted patterning on the Egyptian Mau was not created by deliberate crosses, but has always been there.

According to fans of the breed, the Egyptian Mau is one of the oldest breeds of cat in the world – and a cat that was worshipped in Ancient Egypt.
The illustrations of cats unearthed during excavations in Egypt certainly bear a striking resemblance to the Egyptian Mau. Other people insist that most domestic cats and cat breeds are direct or indirect descendants of the first domesticated Egyptian cats and that the Mau is not exceptional in this respect.

It is known that these cats competed in European and Canadian shows during the nineteenth century and that the first representatives of the breed arrived in the United States from Egypt by way of Italy in the 1950s.

The owner of these cats was a Russian, Princess Nathalie Troubetskoy. She emigrated to the United States and started breeding Silver, Bronze and Smoke Egyptian Maus under the cattery name Fatima. The breed was officially recognized in the United States in 1968, but did not receive recognition in Europe until 1993.

Temperament

The Egyptian Mau is a lively, active cat that loves to play and romp both as a kitten and as an adult cat. Plenty of toys and opportunities to climb are an essential part of the domestic arrangements if your Egyptian Mau is to feel at home.

This breed is not only playful, but also needs a great deal of attention and does not like being left alone for any length of time. These cats love to be stroked and petted and are extremely affectionate; they sometimes become very attached to one particular member of the family.

Silver Egyptian Mau

Spotted Snow Bengal

Clean the ears, if necessary, with a special ear cleaner designed for cats.

Physical characteristics

BODY
The Bengal has a fairly long, muscular, well-

Spotted Snow Bengal

Classic Tabby Snow Bengal kitten

developed body with heavy bones. The hind legs are slightly longer than the front legs and the paws are relatively large and round. The tail is medium-length, feels sturdy and has a rounded tip.

HEAD
The wedge-shaped head is small in relation to the body, and slightly longer than it is wide. The fairly small ears are set slightly forwards; they are wide-spaced and should not be tufted. The nose is long and wide with a slight stop. The eyes are large and almond-shaped to round. Pronounced whisker pads are highly desirable.

COAT
The remarkably dense coat is short to medium-length, smooth and exceptionally soft and silky. Kittens may have a slightly longer coat than adult animals. Bengals may have two sorts of patterning in the coat, spotted and striped, but a very important breed characteristic, irrespective of the coat color or pattern, is the black tip of the tail.

PATTERNS

Spotted
In the spotted marking, it is extremely important for the spots to contrast clearly with the background color. The coat of a spotted Bengal should always have 'vest button' spots, a clear M on the forehead and rings around the tail.

Striped
The striped marking is very much like the classic or blotched marking seen in Oriental

125

Shorthairs, but should have elongated patterns rather than round ones. The striped Bengal also has small round spots on the underparts. A clear contrast and distinct patterning are desirable.

COLORS

Sorrel
The cat has a yellowish to deep orange-red base color, with black, brown, chocolate or cinnamon markings. A clear contrast between the pattern and the background is desirable. The eye color is yellow to green.

Seal Lynx Point
This color variant was obtained by crossing with Siamese. The muzzle, ears and paws are therefore always darker than the rest of the body. However, the points should not be too obvious; the aim is to have the minimum possible color contrast between the points and the rest of the body. The eyes are blue.

Sepia Seal Mink Tabby
This color variant was achieved by crossing Siamese with Burmese. The Sepia Seal Mink Tabby is a relatively rare color. The base color is ivory, cream or light tan. The color of the markings varies from russet to dark brown. The Seal Lynx Point and the Sepia Seal Mink Tabby are sometimes referred to as Snow Bengals. Snow Bengal kittens are usually born with light-colored coats.
Vague markings start to appear after a few weeks. It may take eighteen months for the coat to achieve its ultimate color. The eye color varies from green to blue-green.

Special points

Because the appearance of this breed is not

Spotted Bengal kitten

Classic Tabby Bengal kitten

yet as stable as that of many other breeds, it is not easy to come by a well-marked individual. When you are purchasing a kitten, take a look at the parents. If they have good markings there is a better chance that your kitten will develop similar markings.

Bengals' characters can differ considerably, as well. Character is largely inherited, so if you are looking for an affectionate kitten, choose one whose parents exhibit this trait. The Bengal is not a breed recognized by the CFA in the United States.

Sokoke

The Sokoke is a remarkable breed in many ways. In appearance it falls between a wild cat and an ordinary house cat. Its half-wild but nonetheless affectionate character makes this the ideal pet for people who know the breed. The Sokoke is fairly rare and has only recently been recognized. It is not a recognized breed in the United States according to the largest body of breeder associations.

History

The Sokoke comes from the Sokoke Forest in Kenya. Sokokes lived there for decades before they were discovered. The Sokoke Forest covers an area of about 400 square kilometers (160 square miles) close to the coastal towns of Malindi and Kalifi, about seven kilometers (four miles) from the Indian Ocean.

The forest is effectively isolated and is home to many extraordinary and unique plant and animal species.

Sokoke

into the forest. Jeni was enchanted with her cats and discovered that they had a number of unusual characteristics. They would spend all day in the trees around the house, and yet they showed no interest in birds or their nests – instead they were voracious hunters of insects. Sometimes she saw her cats grazing on the lawn in the evening, just like cattle.

A vet who was visiting Jeni one day told her that he regularly came across cats like these in the Sokoke Forest and had on several occasions tried in vain to catch one of them. According to him they were known as 'white-shouldered cats' and they lived in trees. The tribes that lived in the Sokoke Forest called them 'Khadzonzo,' although the usual word for domestic cats in Kenya is 'Paka.' This confirmed Jeni Slater's belief that she had two very special cats, and so she decided to breed them. A friend of hers, the Canadian Gloria

Sokoke

Jeni Slater and her husband David lived in a house in the village of Watamu, near the Sokoke Forest. Jeni was born and raised in Kenya but is of British descent. One day, while Jeni's gardener was pruning trees, he disturbed a wild cat who was suckling her young. The wild cat ran away, but Jeni had got a good look at her: it was a small cat that looked like the ordinary domestic cats found in Great Britain and elsewhere, but there were a few striking differences. The cat had longer legs and a longer body, large ears and very large, expressive eyes. The cat reminded her of a Cheetah in miniature. The gardener pointed to the litter of kittens, and Jeni decided to adopt a tom and a queen.

The two cats thrived and, because they were so young, rapidly adapted to life as house cats. They made no attempt to escape back

Sokoke

Moldrup, who was living in Denmark, visited Jeni and was bowled over by the cats' unusual looks. Jeni let her take two kittens from different litters back with her to Denmark, where she started working for the official recognition of the Sokoke as a breed. She set up a breeding program with a number of other enthusiasts and regularly imported Sokokes from Jeni's cattery to prevent in-breeding.

In 1983 the breed was recognized as an 'experimental breed' under the name African Shorthair. In 1992 the breed finally achieved official recognition and was given the name it is now known by: Sokoke. To prevent in-breeding, Sokoke breeders still import new cats from Kenya.

Temperament

Sokokes have looked after themselves for generations, but they adapt extremely well to life as pets. Sokokes retain their dignity and independence to a certain extent and a new owner will have to earn the trust of a new kitten.

Sokokes are intelligent, playful and active cats. They like to spend a lot of time out of doors and do not mind the rain. They are good swimmers, and many of them will not hesitate to dive into the pond after fish. Sokokes enjoy the company of humans, other cats, and dogs; they are highly sociable. Once the owner has won the cat's trust, he or she will be able to teach it a great deal, such as retrieving pieces of paper, but the Sokoke will work out for itself how to open doors. You can get these cats accustomed to a life indoors, but it is better if you can give them the opportunity to spend time in your yard or in a large outside run.

Care

The Sokoke can be kept in excellent condition with the minimum of grooming. It is enough to brush the coat once a week with a pig-bristle brush and comb it through with a fine comb. You can follow up by polishing with a damp chamois to bring out the shine.

Trim the sharp tips of the claws regularly, using good clippers, and clean the ears – but only when necessary – with a special ear cleaner.

Sokoke

Physical characteristics

BODY

The Sokoke is a medium-sized cat with a long, lithe, muscular body and a well-developed chest.
The legs are long and slender with oval paws; the hind legs are longer than the front legs. The tail is medium length, narrowing towards the tip. The heavy bone structure means that the cat is fairly heavy for its size.

HEAD

The Sokoke's wedge-shaped head is small in relation to the body. The nose is virtually straight and the chin is firm. The ears are medium-sized with rounded tips and set high on the head, so that the cat always looks alert. The oval to almond-shaped eyes are wide-spaced and expressive.

COAT

The Sokoke's resilient coat is very short and glossy, and lies close to the body. There is little if any undercoat.

COLORS

The Sokoke only occurs in classic tabby pattern.

This is always black on a gray to warm golden brown background. At shows, judges like to see agouti bands on the black hairs. Sokokes have amber to light green eyes.

8 Semi-long-haired breeds

Maine Coon

This popular American breed is the largest breed of domestic cat. Toms in particular can grow into substantial animals weighing six or seven kilos (13 to 15 pounds), and there have been instances of males weighing more than ten kilos (22 pounds). The very long tail with its flowing fur and the ear tufts are important breed features in the Maine Coon. This is one of the 'natural' breeds. With many other breeds, breeders endeavor to achieve an ideal set out in the breed standard, but the most important objective in the case of Maine Coons is to preserve the original type.

These cats are therefore not bred in colors that do not occur naturally – the type of colors we might find in the Siamese, for instance. Despite its profuse, semi-long coat, the Maine Coon needs little more in the way of grooming than a short-haired cat.

History

The Maine Coon owes the first part of its name to the state of Maine, where the breed was originally found. 'Coon' is the regular abbreviated form of raccoon, and refers to the cats' flowing, ringed tails, which are reminiscent of the raccoon's tail. The story goes that the inhabitants of Maine once believed that the Maine Coon was the result of crosses between cats and raccoons. Nowadays, of course, we know that such crosses are genetically impossible. A more plausible explanation is that the ancestors of the Maine Coon were brought by seamen. It was (and still is) customary to take cats on long sea voyages to help keep the rats and mice down on board the ship. Semi-longhairs could have arrived in North America with seafarers from England (Angoras and the forerunners of the Persian Longhair) or from Scandinavia

Left: Silver Black Tabby Maine Coon

White Maine Coon with blue eyes

(Norwegian Forest Cats). Once there, they would have mated with the local short-haired cats. This makes it possible that the Maine Coon may be related to the Norwegian Forest Cat, and almost certain that it is related to the Turkish Angora, the cat we know as one of the ancestors of the Persian Longhair.

Maine Coons appeared in cat shows in the United States, where a cat of this breed won the 'Best Cat' title at the very first major cat show held in this country, as early as 1895. The Maine Coon was a very popular breed around that time, until the British introduced the Persian Longhair to America. These cats looked much more exotic, so cat lovers turned to them and from then on there were far fewer Maine Coons at shows. Their popularity as pets and as the scourge of

133

Golden Black Tabby Maine Coon

Cream Tabby and White Maine Coon

vermin remained undiminished, however, particularly in and around the state of Maine.

In 1951 various breeders and cat lovers picked up the threads again, and the first breed association for the Maine Coon – the Central Maine Cat Club – was founded in the same year. The club started to organize shows exclusively for Maine Coons. People in other countries soon started to show an interest in the breed, and the Maine Coon became a familiar and welcome visitor to shows in Europe. In the early years, breeders in Germany were the major influence on the breeding of the Maine Coon. Despite their efforts, the breed standard was not drawn up

Red Tabby Maine Coon

Black Silver Tabby Maine Coon

until 1967 and it was another ten years before the breed was recognized by the majority of cat associations.

Nowadays, the Maine Coon enjoys great popularity among exhibitors and breeders, and with the general public. It is not uncommon for a Maine Coon to be named 'Best Cat' at a cat show.

Temperament

Maine Coons are uncomplicated, friendly and good-humored cats. Generally speaking, they get along well with other cats and, providing they get acquainted at an early age, they usually have no problems with dogs. Maine Coons are extremely friendly towards adults and children.

They are highly adaptable, and will make themselves equally at home in the country or in a top-floor apartment in the city. If you do want to keep a Maine Coon in an apartment, you must make sure that the cat has plenty of opportunities to play so that it does not get bored. Maine Coons are very playful and inquisitive as kittens, and will not change all that much when they grow up. Because they love to climb and scramble, a sturdy cat gym is a good investment. Although the Maine Coon loves a good game and a romp, there are times when it can be a very quiet and even lazy cat that will love to spend the evening curled up on your lap. Most enjoy being stroked and petted, and will regard a weekly

Maine Coon kitten

grooming session as a pleasant break in the routine. Maine Coons are not noisy, but they will use their voices if they want to tell you something.

Care

The Maine Coon's semi-long coat is self-cleaning and will normally stay in excellent condition if simply brushed once a week. It is advisable to use a pure bristle brush, because synthetic brushes often generate an electro-static charge. You can use a coarse comb in areas where the coat is more profuse and it is difficult to use a brush, but do set about this carefully since it is easy to damage the coat.

The cat will shed in the spring and summer, when the long hair of the mane in particular, will be shed. Obviously you will have to pay more attention to coat care during this

Red-shaded Cameo Maine Coon

Blue Tortie and White Maine Coon

Maine Coon kittens at four weeks old

period, to prevent your cat from ingesting too much hair during its own daily grooming sessions. A rubber brush is a useful aid here, but one drawback is that overly-enthusiastic use can damage the cat's coat. This is why many people who regularly show their Maine Coons prefer simply to brush their cats more often with a soft brush during the shedding season. A Maine Coon that puts in regular

appearances at shows will therefore need more grooming than one that is kept solely as a pet.

Although these cats are not groomed for a show in the way that is customary and essential for a Persian, it will sometimes be necessary to shampoo the coat a week before the show, or even earlier. Because the coat needs time to recover, it is not wise to bathe the cat just before a show. Use only a shampoo formulated especially for cats, because other shampoos have too harsh an effect on the skin's natural oils. You might prefer to powder the cat with an unscented grooming powder a day or two before the show. Sprinkle a little of the powder into the coat and rub it in gently. The dirt and excess grease in the coat adhere to the powder, which you can then brush out with a soft brush.

Only clean the ears when necessary. Use a special ear cleaner for cats, which you

Maine Coon kitten

Black Tortie Tabby and White Maine Coon

Blue Smoke Tortie Maine Coon

Maine Coon kittens at four weeks old

the sharp tips of the claws with a good pair of clippers just before a show.

Physical characteristics

BODY

The Maine Coon is the largest breed of domestic cat: males in particular can grow to be very big. The muscular body is longer than it is tall, with a deep chest.

The well-muscled legs are average length, and the large, round paws have tufts of hair between the toes. Another typical character-istic of the Maine Coon is the long tail, which when laid along the back must reach at least to the neck.

HEAD

The head is of average width, with high cheekbones. The strong chin forms a straight line with the nose and upper lip. Viewed in profile the nose shows a slight curve but certainly not a pronounced stop.

massage gently into the ear and then dab off with a tissue.

You can also use cotton swabs, provided that you are aware of the danger of pushing the dirt further into the ear canal – something that can have unpleasant consequences.
Always take care when using aids like this. Some exhibitors make a practice of trimming

The ears are large and wide at the base. They are high on the head, set well apart and taper to a point.

A typical feature are the ear tufts that curl out from the inside of the ear. Lynx tufts (little plumes on the top of the ear) are highly desirable. The large eyes are slightly oval and slanting.

Blue Tabby Maine Coon

COAT

The Maine Coon has a dense, semi-long coat, with noticeably longer fur on the underparts, flanks and tail. A mane is desirable. The texture of the flowing coat depends on the color: cats with silver factor, non-agouti and dilute colors have softer coats. A short coat or fur the same length all over the body will cost a cat marks at shows.

The coat is usually considerably shorter in the summer than in the winter, but the hair on the tail always remains long and flowing. The kittens can be recognized as semi-longhairs at an early age, but their coats will be far less abundant than those of their parents. The coat is not fully developed until the cat is eighteen months to two years old – and in some cases it may take even longer than this.

COLORS

The Maine Coon is bred only in the 'natural' colors found in ordinary domestic cats. This means that they occur in a great many different coat colors and markings, such as black, blue, red and cream, sometimes with white markings, a tabby pattern or a silver undercoat. The distribution of the color – considered an important aspect in other breeds – is of secondary interest in the Maine Coon. Breeders can concentrate on breeding the correct type of cat with a coat of the right texture and length. A cat that is outstanding in terms of type but has a less elegant distribution of colors will consequently do better at shows than an animal with beautifully symmetrical markings but a poorer quality coat or conformation. The eye color is likewise not regarded as particularly important: Maine Coons may have green, yellow-green, copper and even odd eyes. White Maine Coons with blue eyes are a rarity. Black Classic or Black Mackerel Tabby with White is the most usual color.

Special points

The Maine Coon is slow to develop and will not reach full maturity until it is at least three years old.

Norwegian Forest Cat

The Norwegian Forest Cat, known in its home country as the Norsk Skoggkatt, is very similar to the Maine Coon and is consequently often confused with it. The main physical difference between the two breeds lies in the shape of the head. The Maine Coon has a longer, squarer muzzle and a curving profile, while the Norwegian Forest Cat has a more triangular head and a straight nose. The Norwegian Forest Cat's fur tends to be slightly coarser and greasier. There are also minor differences in character. The Maine Coon is generally more even-tempered. The Norwegian Forest Cat, like the Maine Coon and the Turkish Angora, is one of the natural breeds, which means that they are only bred in the colors found in the wild. The Himalayan pattern we see in the Siamese or the Birman and colors like lilac and chocolate are not recognized for these breeds. The growing popularity of the Maine Coon has meant a

Blue Tortie Tabby and White Maine Coon

degree of reflected interest in the Norwegian Forest Cat. While the Norwegian Forest Cat was relatively unknown just a few decades ago, it is now a regular sight on the show bench and more and more breeders are taking it up.

History

Scientists agree that the origin of long-haired cats is to be found in Southern Russia, Turkey and Iran (formerly Persia). In the past, all cats found outside these areas were short-haired. The ancestors of the Norwegian Forest Cat must therefore have arrived in Norway as a result of man's intervention.

It is assumed that the seafaring Vikings took long-haired cats they found in Turkey and elsewhere back to Scandinavia with them in about the ninth century. Their reason for doing this had nothing to do with any particular admiration for these cats' looks, it was a purely pragmatic desire to keep the vermin under control on board their ships on their long sea voyages.

We can therefore argue that the Norwegian Forest Cat is a distant descendant of the breed we now call the Turkish Angora. Both breeds have a wedge-shaped head and a straight nose, so that this theory is quite plausible. The Norwegian Forest Cat is stockier and the coat is much coarser, but this could be the result of more or less natural selection and the influence of the short-haired cats already living in Scandinavia. The cats with thicker fur and a sturdier build obviously stood a much better chance of surviving the harsh Scandinavian winters than their more delicately built cousins with a less lavish coat.

In light of the numerous references to long-haired cats with plumed tails – Huldrekatten – in old Norse legends, it is thought that the forefathers of the present day Norwegian Forest Cat have lived in the forests of Norway for many centuries. In winter, when the cats

Black Tabby and White Norwegian Forest Cat

had difficulty finding enough food, they would seek human company.

They made themselves extremely useful in and around the houses and farms by destroying vermin, and were consequently highly valued by the people.

A Norwegian Forest Cat was shown as a pedigree cat for the first time in 1912. This was a cat with a black and silver coat and the impressive name of Gabriel Scott Solvfaks.

A group of cat lovers started to develop an interest in the national breed, and this resulted in the formation of an association which set for itself the goal of stabilizing the breed. The breeding program met with varying success and the Norwegian Forest Cat was not officially recognized by the international cat associations until 1977.

Nowadays, the Norwegian Forest Cat is a familiar sight at shows all over the world, but back in the vast Norwegian forests and in the countryside there are still plenty of Norwegian Forest Cats living in the wild.

Temperament

Norwegian Forest Cats have an easy-going, tolerant, sociable nature. They are placid, equable cats, but nonetheless fairly active. Although the name might lead you to think otherwise, this is not a wild, outdoor cat. For centuries many of its ancestors have been cherished pets in the farming communities of Norway. There are many Norwegian Forest Cats that lead a happy life as indoor cats, although it is obviously great for any cat to be able to enjoy itself in a large outdoor run. However, if these cats are kept indoors from birth they really do not miss being able to roam because they have never known anything else. This is not to imply that Norwegian Forest Cats are indolent animals: they are active and playful and must be given

Black Tabby and White Norwegian Forest Cat

the opportunity to work off their energy. Norwegian Forest Cats can climb very well and love to demonstrate their prowess, which means a good scratching and climbing post is absolutely essential. They also really enjoy toys such as fur mice and ping pong balls. These intelligent cats are extremely friendly to adults and children. They like to be stroked and petted, although they are not as forbearing as some of the other longhairs and semi-longhairs and will certainly let it be known if there is anything they do not like. Norwegian Forest Cats have a tendency to become particularly attached to one person. Although they like attention, they are not generally talkative and will not pester you. There are seldom any problems with dogs – in fact there are plenty of instances of lifelong friendships between dogs and Norwegian Forest Cats. Norwegian Forest Cats have a very strong sense of territory, so toms are unlikely to get on well together. Neutered males will usually live together without too many problems. Females, whether they are neutered or not, generally get on well

Black Mackerel Tabby and White Norwegian Forest Cat

together provided that each animal has enough space. This is in striking contrast to the Siamese, for example, who love to sleep curled up together. Above all, Norwegian Forest Cats are inquisitive: they want to know what is going on around them and will subject everything that comes into the house – from a bag of groceries to a visitor – to a thorough inspection.

Cream Norwegian Forest Cat

Black Mackerel Tabby and White Norwegian Forest Cat

Black and White Norwegian Forest Cat

Norwegian Forest Cats have water-repellent, insulating fur that is extremely well adapted to a harsh, wet climate.

They can be kept in an outdoor run summer and winter alike provided they are given enough attention. Most Norwegian Forest Cats will remain playful until they are quite old.

Care

The greasy, water-repellent coat so typical of the breed does not need extensive grooming. Like the other semi-longhair natural breeds, Norwegian Forest Cats need little coat care.

Outside the shedding season, all you need do is tidy the coat every now and then with a coarse comb or a brush, taking great care not to pull too much of the undercoat out. Use a natural bristle brush, never a synthetic one, because synthetic brushes often generate an electrostatic charge.

Norwegian Forest Cats get on very well with other animals.

The Norwegian Forest Cat undergoes a relatively short but heavy shedding season, leaving it looking like a short-haired cat with a long, plumed tail. You will find loose hairs all over the house, but the dead undercoat hair can also become trapped in the coarser guard hairs of the topcoat, where it can cause matting and tangles that are difficult to get out.

The cat will also swallow a lot of hair during its own grooming sessions. It is therefore well worthwhile to brush and comb the cat's coat every day during the spring.

Although it is customary to bathe many of the longhair and semi-longhair breeds before a show, this is highly inadvisable with the Norwegian Forest Cat. Washing makes the coat softer and silkier, ruining the desirable rugged, greasy coat, typical of the breed, for a very long time. The cat will also get dirty more quickly because the shampoo also removes the dirt-repellent layer from the coat.

Only clean the ears when necessary. Use a special ear cleaner for cats, which you massage gently into the ear and then dab off with a tissue. You can also use cotton swabs, provided that you are aware of the danger of pushing the dirt further into the ear canal – something that can have unpleasant consequences.

Always take care when using aids like this. Some exhibitors make a practice of trimming the sharp tips of the claws with a good pair of clippers just before a show.

Physical characteristics

BODY

The Norwegian Forest Cat is a fairly large, sturdy cat with a strong bone structure and a long body. It is a tall cat, with hind legs that are longer than the forelegs, so that the back slopes up slightly towards the tail. The paws are large, round and strong, with tufts of hair between the toes.

The hind legs are completely straight and should never toe out, but the front paws do turn out slightly. The tail is long and thick, with profuse hair.

When the tail is laid along the back it should reach to the hollow between the shoulder blades. Characteristics that will be considered as faults at shows include a frame that is too small, too lean or too long, a short tail or short legs. Males should be somewhat larger and stockier than females.

Blue Mackerel Tabby Norwegian Forest Cat

HEAD

Viewed face on, the head forms an equilateral triangle. The nose is straight and there should not be a stop. The chin is strong but not as clearly pronounced as in the Maine Coon. The almond-shaped eyes are expressive and slightly slanted. In young cats the eyes may still be quite round. The ears are fairly broad at the base and set high on the head; they taper to a point. Viewed from the front, the outer edges of the ears are in line with the shape of the skull, so that the ears and the face form a triangle. There are lynx tufts on the tips of the ears and tufts of longer hair inside the ears, curling slightly backwards. The lynx tufts are not compulsory.

COAT

The quality of the coat is of the utmost importance when showing the Norwegian Forest Cat. It is semi-long with a dense, woolly undercoat. The smooth, shining guard

Black Mackerel Tabby and White Norwegian Forest Cat kitten

Cat, breeders can concentrate on preserving a healthy cat of an attractive type. Black Classic Tabby and Black Mackerel Tabby with and without White are the most usual colors. The Norwegian Forest Cat's eyes may be of any color, ranging from green and yellow to copper and blue. Odd-eyed Norwegian Forest Cats do occur, but they are rare.

Special points

hairs have a water-repellent texture that protects the cat from the weather. Except in the summer, the cat should have a luxuriant mane and bib, and it should always have a long plumed tail.

Obviously cats that spend a lot of time outdoors will have a thicker, denser coat than those who stay indoors, and males have a thicker coat than females. A dry or felt-like coat is regarded as a fault at shows.

COLORS
The Norwegian Forest Cat is only recognized in natural colors, which means it must be a color found in ordinary domestic cats. The Himalayan pattern found in Siamese and Birmans is not permitted, nor are non-natural colors such as lilac, cinnamon and chocolate. In contrast to breeds such as the Persian, little importance is attached to the distribution of the color on the Norwegian Forest Cat's body. Because the distribution of the color and the colors themselves are of secondary interest in the Norwegian Forest

The kittens are recognizable as semi-long-hairs at an early age, but their coat will not be nearly as luxuriant as their parents'. It can take two years or more for the Norwegian Forest Cat to develop its full coat, and it may be as long as three years or more before it reaches its ultimate size.

Siberian Forest Cat

Siberian Forest Cats are very similar in both appearance and character to Norwegian Forest Cats and Maine Coons. The breed is less well known, however, and is consequently not as popular as it perhaps deserves to be.

It is rarely found outside Russia and the former East Bloc countries and is not a breed recognized by the CFA.

The ear tufts and the glossy, semi-long coat are characteristic of the breed. The head is distinctly more round and shorter than that of the Norwegian Forest Cat and the Maine Coon.

History

Little is known about the origins of the Siberian Forest Cat. In all probability these attractive semi-longhairs have lived in Siberia for centuries. It is only recently, however, that they have been discovered by cat fanciers.

The ancestors of the Siberian Forest Cat could have been Angoras or Norwegian Forest Cats, which mated with native short-haired domestic farm cats.

Temperament

In terms of character, the Siberian Forest Cat is very much like the Norwegian Forest Cat.

Siberian Forest Cats are also enthusiastic and accomplished climbers. A good climbing and scratching post will therefore always be a worthwhile investment if you acquire one of these cats. Although Siberian Forest Cats love attention and enjoy being stroked and groomed, they will not usually appreciate over-familiar cuddling.

They retain their dignity under any and all circumstances. They generally get on well

Red and White Siberian Forest Cat

with other cats and dogs, and they are extremely good with children.

Care

Caring for your Siberian Forest Cat's coat should not take up too much of your time because the cat has a water- and dirt-repellent coat that is effectively self-cleaning. When the cat is not shedding, you can brush the coat through about once a week and then comb the areas that are prone to mat and tangle, including behind the ears, between the fore and hind legs and on the chest. Take care not to drag too much hair out of the undercoat.

Like the Norwegian Forest Cat, the Siberian Forest Cat goes through a short but heavy shedding period in spring and early summer. The cat will shed a great deal of hair in a short

Blue Tortie and White Siberian Forest Cat kitten

space of time, and the hair coming out of the undercoat can easily become entangled in the heavier guard hairs. It is therefore essential to brush and comb the coat more frequently during this period. It is unwise to bathe these cats for a show, because this removes the water- and dirt-repellent layer – a breed characteristic – from the coat. It is much better to powder the cat with an unscented grooming powder and then brush it out thoroughly until not a trace is left in the coat. This powder is available from most good pet shops and you can usually get it at cat shows, as well.

Clean the ears if necessary, using an ear cleaner especially formulated for cats. Clip the sharp tips off the claws regularly with good clippers.

Physical characteristics

BODY
The Siberian Forest Cat is a medium-sized,

Black Mackerel Tabby and White Siberian Forest Cat

muscular cat. The body is slightly longer than it is tall. The neck is short and well-muscled, and the strong legs are medium length. There must always be tufts of hair between the toes. The tail is broad and powerful at the base, with a slightly rounded tip. When laid along the back, the tail should reach at least to the shoulder blades. Cats with hind legs that are noticeably longer than the forelegs and cats that are as long as they are tall will lose marks at shows. Fine-boned animals, those with a

Black Silver Tabby Siberian Forest Cat

Black Silver Spotted Tabby Siberian Forest Cat kitten

Blue and White Siberian Forest Cat

long, thin neck or without the tufts of hair between the toes will likewise not get far on the show bench.

HEAD

A short, blunt triangular head is the ideal for this breed. The nose is broad and slightly concave, but there may definitely not be a stop.

The cheeks are strong and massive and the chin should be firm and pronounced. The ears are medium-sized and should be set at least one ear's width apart. The tips of the ears are rounded, with lynx tufts, and there are visible ear furnishings. These cats have large, oval, wide-spaced eyes.

COAT

The Siberian Forest Cat has a semi-long to long coat with a dense undercoat and longer, water-repellent, oily guard hairs. The coat is usually noticeably shorter on the shoulder blades.

COLORS

The Siberian Forest Cat may have any color of coat. The breed is not restricted to the

'natural' colors considered desirable for the Norwegian Forest Cat and the Maine Coon – the Himalayan factor and colors like chocolate and lilac are also found in the Siberian Forest Cat, although these colors are not recognized by every cat association.

The presence or absence of white in the coat and the symmetry of the markings are of secondary importance in the Siberian Forest Cat.

More weight is given to the conformation, the shape of the head and the texture of the coat.

Black Tortie and White Siberian Forest Cat kitten

Black Tortie and White Siberian Forest Cat kitten

Common colors are red, black and dilute forms of these two (cream and blue) either with or without a silver undercoat. These may be self-colors or with agouti, creating Classic Tabby, Mackerel Tabby and Spotted Tabby coats. Tortie and tortoiseshell with agouti (Tortie Tabby) are also permitted.

Siberian Forest Cats with a Van pattern are seldom found, and pure white cats are also rare. Siberian Forest Cats have amber or green eyes, with the exception of the Vans and the White Siberian Forest Cats, which may have blue eyes or odd eyes. Cats of this breed with the Himalayan factor are referred to as 'Neva Masquerade.'

Turkish Angora

The Turkish Angora takes its name from the Turkish capital, Ankara, which used to be known as Angora. It is one of the oldest breeds of cat, and possibly the oldest of the semi-long-haired breeds. Oddly enough, it is only recently that the breed has started to attract interest again. These semi-long-haired, appealing cats are gradually finding more fans among cat lovers and breeders. They are exceptionally attractive cats with an intelligent look. Turkish Angoras are bred in many colors, but white is the traditional color. The silky, semi-long coat is a characteristic of the breed. Together with the Norwegian Forest Cat, the Maine Coon and the Siberian Forest Cat, the

Turkish Angora is one of the natural semi-long-haired breeds.

History

It is said that the first Turkish Angoras seen in Europe were brought from Turkey by Italian merchants at the beginning of the seventeenth century.

These semi-long-haired, elegant cats almost all had white coats and either blue or yellow eyes. Because they looked so exotic – very unlike the short-haired farm cats that Europeans were familiar with – they were often presented as valuable gifts to highly placed and aristocratic patrons. The Turkish Angoras of the period were treated with great respect and they were extremely popular with well-to-do Europeans. The French Court was particularly fond of them and many of these cats were kept there.

White Turkish Angora

White Turkish Angora kitten

White Turkish Angora kitten

the forebears of the cats now bred in Europe and the United States. To this very day, breeders still import animals from their country of origin. The earliest imports were almost all white. They, of course, also produced colored descendants.

In the United States, and later in Europe, the white variety was the first to be recognized. As with all other breeds, it is better not to mate white cats together in order to avoid deafness in the progeny.

Temperament

Turkish Angoras are active, extroverted cats with a very sociable attitude towards people. Their intelligence becomes clear when they set their hearts on something: they will very soon work out how to open kitchen cupboards. This is probably a result of their very inquisitive nature. Everything that

Black Tortie Harlequin Turkish Angora

At the end of the nineteenth century breeders started crossing Turkish Angoras with other cats, and the animals that were produced proved to be even more elegant. These crosses, the predecessors of the Persian Longhairs, slowly but surely ousted the Turkish Angoras from what had seemed to be an unassailable position. They were increasingly pushed into the background and the breed came close to dying out. Between 1910 and 1920 the breed was at an all-time low, because there were very few purebred individuals left anywhere, even in Turkey.

The Turks were very fond of their white cats, and set up a breeding program at the zoos in Ankara and Istanbul to preserve the breed from extinction. It was forbidden to export Angoras, but foreigners occasionally succeeded in getting a purebred cat by illegal means.

In the 1950s, some American breeders succeeded in importing a few cats who became

150

Black Tortie Turkish Angora

Turkish Angoras are capable of giving a great deal of love and devotion, but they expect equal attention in return. You should never leave your Turkish Angora alone in a separate room or outside run for too long. If you are out a lot, you would be wise not to get a Turkish Angora – or to get two so that they can keep each other company.

They generally get on very well with other cats, and seldom have problems with dogs. There are, however, Turkish Angoras that become so attached to 'their' people that they find it hard to share them with other cats, although this is by no means the rule. These elegant cats have a straightforward and equable nature and normally get on well with children. However, if they are treated too roughly they will certainly let this be known, even though they will not rebuff the children too unkindly.

comes into the house – from a bag of groceries to a visitor – will be thoroughly sniffed and examined. Turkish Angoras are playful and adventurous: ping pong balls and other toys will be appreciated.

These cats are very fond of human company, and may form a strong attachment to one particular person. Many of them develop the habit of welcoming their chosen member of the family home with a soft, polite cry.

Turkish Angoras can be trained to walk on a lead, and there are some that will retrieve pieces of paper and other small toys without being taught.

Black Tortie and White Turkish Angora

Care

The Turkish Angora's coat is not prone to matting and can be kept in good condition with a minimum of grooming. Like most cats, Turkish Angoras are generally clean and fastidious, and a weekly session with a bristle brush is enough. If you like, you can run a coarse comb through the coat now and then to tidy it.

When the cat is shedding, a special rubber brush is ideal for removing loose, dead hairs from the coat, but use it with care because you could inadvertently damage the coat if you are too enthusiastic. Turkish Angoras have a relatively light coat in summer, and people who do not know better may mistake them for shorthairs.

If you want to show your Turkish Angora, it may be necessary to bathe it – particularly if it is white. Use a good cat shampoo and do not

bathe it less than a week before the show date, because the coat needs time to settle down again. You could also choose to clean the coat with unscented grooming powder. Sprinkle a little powder into the cat's coat and massage it in gently. The powder will pick up dirt and excess grease and you can then brush it out with a soft brush.

Turkish Angora

Cream Mackerel Tabby Turkish Angora

Blue Tortie and White Turkish Angora

Blue Mackerel Tabby and White Turkish Angora

Blue Mackerel Tabby and White Turkish Angora

Some exhibitors make a practice of trimming the sharp tips of the claws with a good pair of clippers just before a show.

Physical characteristics

BODY

The Turkish Angora is a strong and muscular, but at the same time lithe and elegant, small to medium-sized cat. It has a fine bone structure. The body is relatively long and the hind legs are a little longer than the forelegs, so that the back slopes up slightly towards the tail. Turkish Angoras have small, round paws with tufts between the toes. The neck is slender, graceful and moderately long. The tail is well-plumed and broad at the base, tapering slightly to the tip. When the tail is laid along the back, the tip of the tail must reach at least to the hollow between the shoulder blades, and preferably even further.

Only clean the ears when necessary. Use a special ear cleaner for cats, massage gently into the ear and then dab off with a tissue. You can also use cotton swabs, provided that you are aware of the danger of pushing the dirt further into the ear canal – something that can have unpleasant consequences. Always take care when using aids like this.

Black Silver Spotted Tabby Turkish Angora

Turkish Angora are excellent climbers.

Black Smoke Turkish Angora

Black Spotted Tabby Turkish Angora

Turkish Angoras are not fully grown until they are about two years old.

HEAD

The wedge-shaped head is small to medium-sized in proportion to the body. The long, pointed, tufted ears are set high on the head.

The eyes are large, almond-shaped and slightly slanting. The medium-length nose is slightly concave but may certainly not have a stop. The chin should not be too large.

COAT

The close-lying, semi-long coat is very fine and silky. Turkish Angoras have a plumed tail, a mane and knickerbockers.

COLORS

The most traditional color for the Turkish Angora is white – until recently the only color recognized for the breed. Nowadays the Turkish Angora's coat may be any color or color combination provided they are natural colors. Non-natural colors such as lilac, chocolate, and the Himalayan pattern are not permitted.

The most popular colors are red, black and dilutions of these colors (cream and blue). These may be self-colors or with agouti, creating Classic Tabby, Mackerel Tabby and Spotted Tabby coats. Tortie and tortoiseshell with agouti (Tortie Tabby) are also common colors in this breed.
White markings are permitted with all colors, as is a predominantly white coat with a few spots. Silver undercoats are also accepted.

Turkish Angoras' eyes may be of any color, ranging from green and yellow to copper and blue. White Turkish Angoras with odd eyes are relatively common.

Special points

This breed should not be confused with the

Red and White Turkish Angora kitten

Black Silver Tortie Tabby and White Turkish Angora

Red Turkish Angora kitten

Red Turkish Angora kitten

Angora cat bred in Britain – which is still known as the Angora in Britain and the United States, and as the Oriental Semi-longhair elsewhere.

Turkish Van

The Turkish Van (pronounced 'varn') is an unusual breed of cat in many respects. The name comes from Lake Van in Turkey. The first two Turkish Vans seen in Europe were brought from this area in 1955. These imports were predominantly white with two patches of color on the head and a colored tail, and since then this coloration, which is also found in other breeds, has been described as the Van pattern. The Van is the only domestic cat breed that will not hesitate to follow its prey into the water. While it might not go swimming for fun, this cat is certainly not afraid of water.

History

The Turkish Van is a natural cat breed that has been able to develop undisturbed, without the intervention of humans, in the foothills of Mount Ararat, in the isolated region around Lake Van in eastern Turkey. History does not tell us how the semi-long-haired animals with their specific characteristics arrived there. It has been suggested that they may be the descendants of semi-long-haired Chinese cats that came to the Lake Van area along the busy Silk Road and stayed there.

In 1955, two friends visiting Lake Van were fascinated by the colorful, semi-longhair feral cats that were so numerous in the area. One of them, an Englishwoman named Laura Lushington, managed to catch two of them and take them back to Britain. These two animals, both predominantly white with the characteristic red markings, attracted a great deal of attention.

The two cats, together with other imports who arrived a few years later, formed the basis for the Turkish Van breed in Europe. The breed was recognized in Britain in 1969 and two years later received official recog-nition from the FIFe on mainland Europe. Turkish Vans are currently also being bred in the United States. The CFA awarded the breed Championship status in 1994.

Temperament

The Turkish Van has an unusual temperament which requires its owner to have some knowledge of the character of cats. Turkish Vans are affectionate and usually very fond of people, but they will let you know in no uncertain terms if they feel they are being unfairly treated. People who know about cats will not find Turkish Vans unpredictable – after all, their body language makes it quite clear that they have had enough of a particular situation – but others less exper-ienced may not understand this. A great deal can be said and written about these cats, but placid and equable they are not! Turkish Vans are inclined to attach themselves

Turkish Van

Turkish Van

Turkish Van

Turkish Van

particularly to one member of the family. All the cat's affection, love and tenderness will be directed towards that person. The other members of the family will be accepted – and the Van will regularly seek their company – but usually the overwhelming expressions of love will be reserved for one, or at the most, two people. Turkish Vans are usually very

The blue-eyed Turkish Van is rare.

sociable with cats and dogs; relations between the animals are generally very good.

Turkish Vans are active cats that love to hunt and play. They are extremely courageous and where another cat may be upset by loud noises or an unexpected reaction on the part of the prey, the Turkish Van will regard this as a challenge to 'sort things out.'

The breed as a whole is not afraid of water so owners of these cats will have to be inventive when it comes to disciplining them. Generally speaking, a well-aimed squirt from a water pistol is enough to call most cats to order, but there is a very good chance that your Turkish Van will regard this as a wonderful and exciting game.

Although relatively few Turkish Vans will actively seek out water in order to go for a swim, a Turkish Van will not hesitate to take the plunge during the course of a hunt. Owners of these cats will tell you that there are some who dive into garden ponds to catch

the fish. Ducks will also be pursued well out into the water.

Owning a Turkish Van is without doubt an extraordinary experience but it is only for people who can allow this cat, with all the idiosyncrasies characteristic of the breed, to be itself.

Turkish Van

Care

Like all semi-longhairs, Turkish Vans require little grooming. The coat is not prone to matting, so it will be enough to tidy it up occasionally with a soft brush or a coarse comb.

Try to get your kitten used to this in an enjoyable way at an early stage, because if you leave it too long a grooming session will almost inevitably end in a wrestling match. If you want to show your Turkish Van, it may be necessary to bathe the cat with a good shampoo formulated especially for cats. Do this about two days before the show, because the fur needs this long to settle down again. Shampoo not only removes the dirt from the coat, it also has the tendency to remove the natural oils, leaving the hair straighter and lanker, so that it stands away from the body. A lot of owners consequently prefer not to risk this. Instead they clean the cat's coat with unscented grooming powder the day before the show.

When the powder is massaged gently into the cat's coat, dirt and excess grease will stick to it. You can then brush it out easily with a soft brush. Clean the ears if necessary, using an ear cleaner especially formulated for cats. Clip the sharp tips off the claws regularly with good clippers, but keep in mind that you will have to get the cat used to this when it is still young.

Physical characteristics

BODY
The Turkish Van is a medium-sized cat with a long, muscular, powerful body. The legs are average length and the paws are elegant and round. The length of the thick tail should be in good proportion to the body.

HEAD
The Turkish Van has a blunt, triangular head. The large eyes are oval and slightly slanted. The ears are set fairly close together and are pricked up alertly.

Turkish Van

COLORS
The Turkish Van's body is predominantly white. The ideal is two markings on the head, preferably leaving the eyes and ears free, with a white blaze between them, and a colored tail.

A cat with an additional mark on its body will not be penalized at shows. A single mark on the head and markings that are not entirely symmetrical are also permitted. A good type is more important than a spot more or less.

The Turkish Van is usually either Red or Cream – black, blue, tortoiseshell and tabby markings also occur, but they have not yet been recognized everywhere. Most Vans have amber eyes, but some are odd-eyed or have blue eyes.

Turkish Van

guardians of the Temple of Lao Tsun. The golden goddess of the temple had deep blue eyes. When the temple was attacked and the head priest was killed, his cat is said to have placed his feet on his master and to have faced the goddess: its fur took on a golden cast, its eyes turned as blue as those of the goddess, and its face, legs and tail turned the color of the earth. The cat's paws, however, where they touched the priest, remained white as a symbol of purity.

In any event it is clear that various people brought cats resembling Birmans back with them from Burma around the turn of the century. It is largely due to the French cat fanciers that the breed was introduced in Europe and later in the United States. The fact that France played a major role in the popularization of the Birman is easy to prove, because the pedigrees of all Birmans ultimately lead back to France. Critics say that French breeders actually created the Birman themselves by crossing various other

Seal Point Birman kitten

Birman

The Birman (often described as the 'Sacred Cat of Burma') is a striking semi-longhair with an exotic look. It is probably true to say that no other breed is the subject of so many conflicting opinions and stories about its origins. The white paws and legs are the typical breed characteristic. Birmans are only bred in the Himalayan pattern (with points) and always have blue eyes. These cats are generally gentle and intelligent creatures that get on well with everyone.

History

The origins of this breed are the subject of the most charming and imaginative stories. One of the best-known, which can of course be consigned to the realm of fable, is that for centuries these cats were yellow-eyed and white, living in a Burmese monastery as the

160

Blue Tortie Tabby Point Birman

Seal Tabby Point Birman

Birman can live with dogs providing it is not chased by them, because it does not find this amusing.

Birmans have a reputation as picky eaters, but this probably has a lot to do with the fact that many owners of these cats are inclined to spoil them; it is certainly not a breed characteristic. These cats are not usually very vocal and will attempt to let you know what

Blue Tortie Tabby Point Birman

breeds, and then surrounded them with these romantic stories to increase demand. There is no question that domestic cats with white socks, Siamese and Colorpoint Persians were used in the early years of the French breeding program.

Temperament

As a rule, Birmans are gentle, serene, shy and tolerant. They like peace and quiet, and you must give them the opportunity to go off quietly by themselves from time to time. They are not really suited to a boisterous environment, which could upset their equilibrium. Birmans like company and need a fair amount of contact with the other members of the family if they are to be happy. Some Birmans have a tendency to turn into a one-person cat, selecting one member of the family with whom they form a real bond. They usually get on well with other cats. A

Seal Tabby Point Birman

Seal Point Birman

Birman kittens

Birman kittens

they want by nuzzling up to you and trying to establish eye contact. Despite their placid nature, most of them will enjoy a game and a romp occasionally, but they will certainly not treat your home like a playground.

Care

The Birman's soft, semi-long and extremely dense coat needs relatively little grooming. The texture is such that the coat rarely becomes matted. Generally speaking, a weekly brushing session will keep a Birman's coat in good condition. Whatever you do, do not use a metal comb on your cat, because this can damage the undercoat. A stiff bristle brush is much better. If you plan to show your Birman, it will require a good deal more in the way of grooming because the judges attach a great deal of weight to the quality of the coat. Some people bathe the cat a day or two before the show, but seasoned exhibitors

Blue Point Birman

advise against this. The shampoo leaves the coat too soft and fluffy on the day of the show. They recommend bathing the cat about five days prior to a show. After this you can powder the coat regularly, as is done with breeds such as the Turkish Angora and the Maine Coon.

Ear tufts are not considered desirable at shows, so trim them off very carefully, and you should of course make sure that the cat's ears are clean. Sharp points on the claws should be trimmed with a good, strong pair of clippers.

Physical characteristics

BODY
The Birman is a medium-sized, well-proportioned cat. The tail is medium-length in proportion to the rest of the body and should make an elegant impression. The Birman should not be too tall; the legs should be on

Red Point Birman

the short side rather than too long. The paws are round and must have the white 'gloves' and 'gauntlets' characteristic of the breed.

HEAD
The forehead is round and the cheeks are full. The nose is medium-length; there may not be a definite stop, but there should be a slight dip. The chin should be firm but not too pronounced. The ears are set at a slight angle and point forwards. A Birman's eyes should be the deepest possible blue, and oval – they should not be round like a Persian Long-hair's.

COAT
The Birman's coat has a very unusual texture. It is soft and silky, and floats around the cat like a luxuriant veil. The Birman has very little undercoat – under no circumstances should the coat be too thick, and a curly undercoat will lose marks at shows. The coat is longer in the mane, on the tail and around the hind legs.

Seal Point Birman

COLORS
The Birman is only bred in the Himalayan or colorpoint pattern.

The white paws are the most obvious difference between these cats and other colorpoint breeds. This important breed characteristic must always be present. The white markings should be as symmetrical as possible, and extend up the back of the leg in a V shape. In all cases, the color on the body should be as

Lilac Point Birman

pure as possible and contrast well with the colored points. The eyes are deep blue, irrespective of the coat color. The Birman can be seal point, blue point, chocolate point, lilac point, red point, cream point, tortie point, tabby point and tortie tabby point. However, the largest body of breed organizations in the United States, the CFA, only recognizes Chocolate Point, Seal Point, Lilac Point and Blue Point.

Special points

As in the case of all other cats with points, Birman kittens are born white and the points develop later. It may take as long as a year for the Birman to develop its definite coat color.

Ragdoll

The Ragdoll is so called because – it is said – the animal flops like a rag doll when it is picked up. It is also asserted that cats of this breed will not fight back in a threatening situation, but will simply put up with whatever happens. And finally they are supposed to have an extremely high tolerance to pain, which can sometimes prove fatal. Unfortunately, there are still all too many people who believe this nonsense. Ragdolls feel pain just like any other cat; it is simply that they are placid and docile by nature and are very resistant to stress. They are also extremely affectionate. The trust they place in people is more likely to be the reason why they put up with a great deal, and why they relax completely when they are picked up, rather than any genetic factor.

History

A persistent myth is that the heavily pregnant forebear of the Ragdoll line was run over by a car.

The dam, a white Persian, survived, but her character underwent a remarkable change. She became exceptionally sweet-tempered

Seal Point Mitted Ragdoll

and her body would go as limp as a rag doll's when she was picked up. The kittens she gave birth to inherited her docile nature. Anyone who knows even a little about genetics will realize that this is absolutely impossible.

A non-purebred white Persian Longhair queen was, however, one of the progenitors of the Ragdoll in California in the 1960s. The sire was a seal point Birman. Ragdolls also have Persian, Burmese and non-pedigree blood.

Lilac Point-White Ragdoll

165

Lilac Point-White Ragdoll kitten

necessarily a problem, because most Ragdolls are perfectly happy to stay indoors.

Ragdolls are extraordinarily sociable and equable animals that are not easily upset. They fit in very well in a lively family with young children, and they will live in harmony with other cats and dogs. In a threatening situation, a Ragdoll's first instinct will be to run away; its claws will only be used as the last possible resort. These cats are very quiet and will rarely use their soft voices.

These gentle, elegant and intelligent creatures like company and love being cuddled and groomed, but it is not in their nature to force themselves on you. They are very inquisitive and interested in everything that goes on around them.

Cats of some of the other breeds may have the occasional bad mood, but most Ragdolls seem to have a perpetually sunny outlook on life.

Care

Temperament

The most striking thing about the Ragdoll is its gentle, quiet and docile nature, and the immense trust it places in people and other animals. It is not advisable to allow Ragdolls to roam free outdoors, because they will simply allow themselves to be taken away by anyone who is nice to them. This is not

The Ragdoll's semi-long, silky coat is not prone to matting and consequently needs relatively little care. A gentle brushing once a week, or a comb through with a coarse comb, is all that is required. During the shedding season, a rubber brush will help you remove loose, dead hair simply and quickly, but be careful because overly enthusiastic brushing will damage the coat. Many exhibitors bathe their Ragdolls a few days prior to taking them to a show, but you might prefer to powder the

Blue Point Ragdoll

Blue Point Ragdoll kitten

coat every so often with an unscented grooming powder. Massage the powder in well so that it can pick up the dirt and excess grease, and then brush it out carefully with a soft brush.

Clean the ears if necessary, using an ear cleaner especially formulated for cats. Clip the sharp tips off the claws regularly with good clippers.

Blue Point Ragdoll

Physical characteristics

BODY
The Ragdoll is a large, muscular but very elegant cat with a long body, a short powerful neck and a deep chest.

The hindquarters are heavier-set and higher than the forequarters. The medium-length legs are heavy-boned, and the paws are large and round with tufts of fur between the toes. The tail is fluffy and in good proportion to the body.

HEAD
The wedge-shaped head is medium size, with well-developed cheeks and a strong chin. The medium-sized ears are reasonably wide-set, with rounded tips. There is a slight dip in the nose, and the large eyes are oval and always blue. Dark blue eyes are particularly desirable for showing purposes.

COAT
The silky coat is of medium length, and the hair of the mane and on the tail is longer than

167

the rest. The hair lies smoothly and does not stand out. The Ragdoll sheds considerably in the summer.

COLORS

Three different varieties of Ragdoll are recognized, and all three are found in seal point, blue point, chocolate point and lilac point. The lighter areas of the coat (with the exception of the white) may become darker over the years as a result of a cold ambient temperature and licking of the fur. The coat may also darken up in places where the skin has been injured. Ragdolls that seldom if ever go outdoors and those that live in a warm climate are therefore likely to be a purer color.

Breeding cats with light-colored coats is particularly difficult in the Seal Point and the Blue Point, because shadowing is very obvious in these colors.

Colorpoint

Colorpoint Ragdolls have a cream body with darker extremities (mask, ears, legs and tail). The chest is usually lighter than the rest of the body. Seal Points and Blue Points have a darker color on the body than the Chocolate Points and Lilac Points. The Colorpoint Ragdoll may not have any white markings.

Mitted

Mitted Ragdolls have a cream body with darker extremities. They differ from the Colorpoints in that they have white 'mittens' on their forepaws and white 'boots' (up to the hock) on their hind legs. The whole underside of the body – of the chin, the chest and the underparts as far as the tail – should also be white.

Bi-color

The Bi-color is the most eye-catching variety: there is no other breed that combines these unique markings with colored points. However, it is by no means easy to breed a Bi-color with the ideal markings. Bi-colors have a white chin, chest and underparts, and the paws are also white.

A very important feature is a white mask in the shape of an inverted V. Ideally, the mask begins in the center of the forehead and runs past the eyes to the back of the chin. White spots on the back are permitted in Bi-color

Ragdolls. As with the other two varieties, the body is cream. The CFA in the United States does not call this variety a Bi-color: instead it adds White to the point name (e.g. Chocolate Point-White).

Special points

Ragdoll kittens are all white when they are born. Their mask, ears, tail and legs darken up later. They are slow to mature and it may take three years before they reach their full adult weight – about five kilos (eleven pounds) for females and eight kilos (eighteen pounds) for males.

Lilac Point-White Ragdoll

Kuril Bobtail

The Kuril Bobtail is extremely rare and is found almost exclusively on the Kuril Islands. The breed has a strikingly short, but plumed tail.

History

The Kuril Bobtail probably descends from a number of Japanese Bobtails. Since 1875 the Kuril Islands have been held by Russia, but prior to this date the islands belonged to Japan. In all probability, the Japanese took their Japanese Bobtails with them to the Kurils where, over the years, some became feral and others maintained an existence as pets.

For a long time, the volcanic and inaccessible Kuril Islands were a strictly guarded military area, and the islanders had little contact with the rest of the world. Comparing the Japanese Bobtail and the Kuril Bobtail, we see that there are no short-haired Kuril Bobtails and they are heavier and stockier.

The cats undoubtedly developed these characteristics over the years because they were useful to them in their inhospitable surroundings.

Following the break-up of the Soviet Union, scientists were able to visit the archipelago, and it was then that they discovered the existence of this breed. Several Kuril Bobtails are now being kept by cat fanciers in Russia, and a pedigree register has even been set up for the breed. These cats are almost unknown outside Russia. Today, Kuril Bobtails still live as feral cats or pets on the Kuril Islands. The breed is not yet recognized by the CFA in the United States.

Temperament

There is a distinct difference between the Kuril Bobtails that come straight from the Islands and the cats bred by cat lovers at home.

The former are obviously much wilder, but both are friendly and good-tempered. Kuril Bobtails are highly adaptable and show their affection without being pushy. They definitely like being petted. They get on exceptionally well with other cats and dogs.

Kuril Bobtail

Kuril Bobtail

Kuril Bobtail

Care

The Kuril Bobtail does not require much grooming. It is enough to brush the coat with a bristle brush or coarse comb once a week to remove loose, dead hair.

The cat will undergo a short but intense shedding season in the spring, and at this time its coat will need more attention. Keep the ears clean with a special ear cleaner, and clip the claws occasionally.

Physical characteristics

BODY
The body is strong, well-muscled and stocky, and the powerful hind legs are longer than the forelegs, so that the back slopes up slightly towards the tail. One interesting characteristic of the breed is the way that it moves in many situations: by creeping forward one paw at a time. The tail, which is about eight centimeters (three inches) long, is held to one side when the cat is at rest and straight up when it is walking or alert. The tail may be kinked, bent or slightly twisted.

HEAD
The Kuril Bobtail has a relatively large, wedge-shaped head with full, well-developed cheeks. The ears are set high on the head, they are medium-sized and have prominent ear furnishings. The nose is medium length with a slight dip. The eyes are large and almond-shaped, with an alert, inquisitive expression and they are slightly slanted. The whiskers and eyebrows are noticeably long.

COAT
The coat is semi-long with little undercoat and a silky feel. The mane and the hair on the underparts and flanks is longer than the hair on the rest of the body. The tail ends in an attractive plume or pom-pom, and there are tufts between the toes.

COLORS
Kuril Bobtails are found in the 'natural' colors such as black and red, with and without white markings and tabby patterning.

Special points

The coat is not fully developed until the cat is about two years old.

Kuril Bobtail

9 Semi-long-haired varieties

British Semi-longhair

British Semi-longhair

British Semi-longhair

Persian Longhairs were originally used and are still used now and again to maintain the round and stocky British Shorthair type. Many British Shorthairs consequently carry the gene for long hair, and when two cats with the long hair gene are mated, some of the kittens in the litter will have a semi-long coat. For many years breeders simply looked for good homes for these kittens, and they were never used for breeding, but a number of the governing bodies have recently recognized the British Semi-longhair as a

Left: Chocolate Somali

separate breed. British Semi-longhairs combine a handsome, stocky conformation with a semi-long coat, and make friendly, placid pets. The breed standard for these cats is the same as for the British Shorthair, with the exception of the length of the coat.

Balinese (long-haired Siamese)

The Balinese is the long-haired counterpart of the Siamese. Its conformation should consequently be exactly the same as that of the Siamese. Their temperaments are very similar as well, although some aficionados of the breed say that they are not quite as strident as their short-haired cousins.

History

The Balinese was first seen in the United States. Some time during the 1950s, a Siamese queen had a litter of kittens which included some with long hair. There are two possible explanations for this.

The gene for long hair is recessive and will always be suppressed by the dominant gene for short hair. It can consequently be carried by short-haired cats for generations and passed on to their progeny without a long-haired kitten ever being born. However, when two short-haired cats, both of which happen to carry the gene for long hair are mated, there is a good chance that at least one of the kittens in the litter will have a long-haired coat. It is highly likely that, somewhere in the dim, distant past, one or more Siamese cats were crossed with a long-haired cat without this having been announced to the world at large. The long hair gene was, however, passed on invisibly through subsequent generations until it finally emerged in the American breeder's litter.

The other explanation is that this was a sudden genetic mutation. Mutations that result in a different hair length or coat texture are far from uncommon – they are what brought about breeds like the Devon Rex and the American Wirehair.

The Balinese has become increasingly well-known and more and more popular. Initially the breed was referred to as the Long-haired

Foreign White Balinese

Siamese, but the name was later changed to Balinese because it was thought that its graceful movements were like those of Balinese dancers. The Balinese was recognized by most of the American cat associations at the beginning of the 1970s, and later by associations in Europe. In the United States, all Balinese must have the classic Siamese colors (Seal, Chocolate, Blue or Lilac Point). Other colors, such as Tabby and Tortie Point, are called Javanese.

Temperament

The Balinese character is very like that of the Siamese. Like Siamese, Balinese are intelligent, lively cats with a very strong personality. Balinese are playful and remain so as they get older. They can amuse themselves all day long with all sorts of cat toys, and will generally make good use of a scratching post. Balinese like the company of people and do not take well to being left alone. If you have to be out a great deal, it is a good idea to get a playmate for your Balinese. Balinese get on well with other cats and, unlike most other breeds, seem to have no need for their own space. If you keep more than one Balinese with other Oriental breeds you will find that the cats love to sleep curled up together in a heap. Since Balinese, like Siamese, love attention, they can be a real nuisance, pestering people at the most inconvenient moments. People who keep this breed say that their cat is as demanding as two (or three) ordinary cats, and anyone who has ever had a Balinese or other Oriental breed will echo this. If Balinese do not get enough attention they will certainly demand it vociferously or express their displeasure in some other way. Balinese are extremely talkative; they like to made their rather raucous voices heard and will carry on conversations with people for hours on end. Because Balinese are so attached to people, they can easily be taught all sorts of tricks, such as fetching wadded-up balls of paper.

Seal Point Balinese

Blue Point Balinese

Foreign White Balinese

Most of them learn remarkably quickly how to walk on a lead.

Care

Unlike many of the other semi-longhair breeds, the Balinese does not have a woolly undercoat, so the coat is relatively easy to keep in good condition. You should brush the coat with a pig-bristle brush about once a week and follow up with a wide-toothed comb. When the cat is shedding, a special rubber brush is ideal for removing loose, dead hairs from the coat, but use it with care because you could inadvertently damage the Balinese's fine coat if you are overly enthusiastic.

If you plan to show your Balinese, you may need to shampoo the coat a few days before the date of the show. You could also opt to powder the cat with an unscented grooming powder, brushing it out again thoroughly. The powder absorbs dirt and excess grease, leaving the coat clean and fresh. Keep the ears clean with a special ear cleaner, which you can get from your vet and from good pet shops, and trim the sharp claws regularly with good clippers.

Physical characteristics

BODY
The Balinese has the same conformation as the Siamese. The muscular body should be long and lithe, with no trace of coarseness anywhere. The hindquarters are higher than the forequarters and the legs are long and slender, with oval paws. The tail is long and thin, and should have no kinks or other irregularities.

HEAD
The head is wedge-shaped. Viewed from the front, the face forms a perfect triangle with the large, diagonally set ears. Strongly developed cheek muscles spoil the lines of the head and are therefore undesirable. The chin should be firm but not too pronounced, and a weak, receding chin is regarded as a serious fault at shows. There must not be any stop in the nose, which should run in a straight line to the forehead. Balinese have slanting, almond-shaped eyes, which should be the purest possible color. At shows judges like to see Balinese with dark blue eyes.

Blue Point Balinese

COAT
The Balinese's semi-long coat is fine and silky, and should lie flat against the skin. A coat that stands out from the body, is too coarse or has too much undercoat will rule a cat out for show purposes. The hair on the tail is long, silky and not too thick in texture.

COLORS
Because the Balinese is a long-haired Siamese, all the colors found in the Siamese are recognized for the Balinese. In the Balinese, like the Siamese, the points (ears, mask, legs and tail) are darker than the rest of the body. Cold, wounds and weather may cause the lighter areas of the coat to darken over the years.

At shows, judges will always prefer Balinese with the purest possible color, preferably without shadows or dark markings on the body.

Seal Point Balinese

Lilac Point Balinese

A great many colors and patterns are recognized, but the ones described below are the most common. For a more detailed description, please turn to the breed description of the Siamese.

Seal and Blue Points
It is far from easy in practice to breed good Seal Point and Blue Point Balinese. These colors almost always have the undesirable shadowing on the coat. This is why most breeders try to breed only from animals in which this effect is not present. Seal and Blue Points may have self-colored, tabby, tortie or tortie tabby points. The points may also have a silver background.

Red and Cream Points
Barring on the legs and rings around the tail are difficult to eliminate from these colors, so that Red and Cream Balinese with solid points are almost impossible to tell apart from Red and Cream Tabby Points.

Chocolate and Lilac Points
Chocolate and the dilute form of this color, Lilac, are very popular colors. The points may be self-colored or they may have tabby, tortie or tortie tabby markings. The points may also have a silver background.

Special points

Balinese kittens are all white when they are born. The typical Himalayan pattern does not start to show up until later.
The coat will take a full year to develop its adult color. Aside from the length of the coat, the standard for the Balinese is identical to the Siamese breed standard. In practice, however, it is the Siamese that conform most closely to the breed standard. Many Balinese breeders therefore make a practice of introducing Siamese blood into their Balinese lines.
The short-haired kittens born as a result of these crosses are referred to as 'variants'; they will carry the recessive long-haired gene. These 'variants' can make a valuable contribution to improving the Balinese type. Breeders of Siamese will seldom if ever take 'variants' into their cattery, partly because these cats may sometimes have a slightly longer coat, which is very undesirable in a Siamese, and partly because they rarely conform as fully to the breed standard as a purebred Siamese (see also Chapter 7, Short-haired breeds, Siamese). The CFA, the largest association of breeder organizations in the United States, recognizes only the Seal, Blue, Chocolate and Lilac Point colors in Balinese; other colors are regarded as Javanese.

Oriental Semi-longhair (Mandarin, Javanese, Angora)

The Oriental Semi-longhair is the semi-long-haired variant of the Oriental Shorthair. This breed has a lot in common with the Balinese, but there are distinct differences in the coat and eye color. Like Oriental Shorthairs, and unlike Balinese and Siamese, Oriental Semi-longhairs do not have points or blue eyes. Oriental Semi-longhairs make excellent pets.

Black Mackerel Tabby Oriental Semi-longhair

remain so for most of their lives. A sturdy scratching post and a good selection of toys will certainly be appreciated. These cats are bright, intelligent and inquisitive, and very little will escape their notice.

They get along extremely well with other Oriental type cats, and they will generally have no problems with other breeds of cat. This breed is very fond of people, which makes it very easy to teach them tricks, such as retrieving a ball of paper.

History

They also take very readily to walking on a lead. Oriental Semi-longhairs need a great deal of attention to keep them happy, and return the love they are given twofold. These are not cats that can be left alone for any length of time. Consider getting two or more Oriental Semi-longhairs so that they can keep one another company.

This appealing breed was created by crossing Oriental Shorthairs and Balinese – the Balinese providing the silky, semi-long coat. Breeders in Great Britain and the United States developed a similar type of Oriental Semi-longhair independently of one another, and this has resulted in different names and different standards for this breed.

Chocolate Oriental Semi-longhair

Temperament

Oriental Semi-longhairs are friendly cats with a very strong personality of their own. They are exceptionally affectionate and love attention, but they can also be wilful. They are talkative and have a strident voice. Oriental Semi-longhairs are playful and

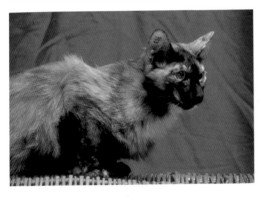

Care

The Oriental Semi-longhair's coat does not have a woolly undercoat, so grooming is not a difficult job. Generally speaking, a weekly session with a pig-bristle brush is enough to keep the coat in good condition.

When the cat is shedding, a special rubber brush is ideal for removing loose, dead hairs from the coat, but use it with care because you could inadvertently damage the Oriental Shorthair's fine coat if you are too enthusiastic. If you are going to show your cat,

Black Mackerel Tabby Oriental Semi-longhair

you may want to bathe it a few days before the show.

With light-colored cats, a bath is essential. You can, however, achieve very much the same effect if you regularly powder the cat with unscented grooming powder and brush it out again thoroughly almost immediately. This powder is available from most good pet shops; it is specially designed to attract dirt and excess grease, so that after one of these beauty treatments the coat looks fresh and well-cared-for again. Use a special ear cleaner to keep the ears clean and trim off the sharp points of the claws regularly using good clippers.

Physical characteristics

BODY
The Oriental Semi-longhair should have the same conformation as the Oriental Shorthair.

The Oriental Semi-longhair has a long, muscular, lithe body. The legs are long, slim and elegant, and the paws are oval. The hindquarters are longer than the forequarters, so that the back slopes up slightly towards the tail.

The tail is long and thin. Oriental Semi-longhairs that are coarse in any respect stand no chance on the show bench.

HEAD
The Oriental Semi-longhair's head is like that of the Oriental Shorthair. It is wedge-shaped, and the face should form a perfect triangle with the large, diagonally-set ears. The chin is firm, but should not be too pronounced. There is no nose break; the long nose runs straight to the forehead. The almond-shaped eyes are slanting, and should have an Oriental expression.

COAT
The cat's semi-long coat has a fine, silky feel, and should lie flat against the skin. The coat may not stand out and must not be too thick. There is virtually no undercoat. The hair on the tail is long and silky.

COLORS
All the colors recognized for the Oriental Shorthair (see Chapter 7, Short-haired breeds, Oriental Shorthair) are found in the

Blue Classic Tabby Oriental Semi-longhair

Oriental Semi-longhair. The most popular are Blue, Havana (brown) and Ebony (black). The eyes should be bright green, preferably without any hint of yellow or amber. White cats may be odd-eyed, in other words with one green and one blue eye.

Special points

It is common to cross Oriental Semi-longhairs with Oriental Shorthairs or Siamese to improve the type. The short-haired kittens that result from these crosses are referred to as 'variants' and carry the gene for long hair.

If two variants are mated together, the statistical probability is that one out of every four kittens will be an Oriental Semi-longhair (see also Chapter 7, Short-haired breeds, Oriental Shorthair).

Chocolate Silver Tabby Oriental Semi-longhair

Lilac Oriental Semi-longhair

Somali (Long-haired Abyssinian)

The Somali is the long-haired version of the Abyssinian. The name is taken from Somalia, in Africa, but the country actually has nothing to do with the origins of this breed. Aficionados of this breed are particularly attracted by the combination of its wild looks and its extremely affectionate nature.

History

Fawn Somali

The Somali cannot claim any ancient, interesting history, but the breed from which the Somali derives – the Abyssinian – is probably one of the oldest breeds in the world.

The name Somali is misleading, because the breed has nothing to do with the country of Somalia. The first Somalis were born in the United States and this is where the most has been done to achieve recognition for the breed. The Somali actually came about by chance. From the start of serious Abyssinian breeding, breeders were occasionally unpleasantly surprised by the appearance of one or more semi-long-haired kittens in a litter of Abyssinians. Initially the little semi-longhairs were simply found good homes, but at a later

Ruddy Somali

Chocolate Somali

Red Silver Somali

Temperament

The Somali's character is very similar to the Abyssinian's. Like the Abyssinian, the Somali is a companionable cat that needs a lot of human contact and attention. It goes against every fibre of its being to spend the whole day alone or to be left on its own in an outside run or separate room – and it will certainly do nothing for the cat's character.

Somalis prefer attention from members of the family, but if you are out they will make do with the company of another cat, or even a dog. You should be aware, however, that females in particular are not always tolerant of other animals – it all depends on the amount of space you have in the house or in the outside run.

Somalis are sociable, and, in general they are reasonably good with children. If the Somali is your first pet and you decide later on to get

stage breeders and cat fanciers started to take an interest in these attractive by-products of their Abyssinians. They decided to carry on breeding the semi-longhair Abyssinians with the aim of creating a new breed. Around the end of the 1960s, the breed was recognized by a number of cat associations. Nowadays the Somali is a familiar and frequent sight at cat shows all over the world.

Two Red Somalis

Chocolate Silver Somali

fairly smooth texture of the coat means that it is not prone to matting. It is best to use a bristle brush to remove the loose hair from the coat.

Every now and then you can comb through the denser parts of the coat with a wide-toothed comb, but do go about this carefully because it is easy to damage the coat. As with all cats, you should clip the claws occasionally with a good pair of clippers and keep the ears clean with an ear cleaner specifically designed for cats.

Physical characteristics

BODY
The Somali's muscular, strong and lean body is moderately long and of intermediate Oriental type. It should not be too large or too coarse, and certainly not stocky. The legs are slim in relation to the body, with a fine

Ruddy Somali

other pets, it is worth knowing that some Somalis can become jealous when they no longer receive the amount of attention they are used to.

Somalis are extroverted animals who definitely make their presence felt, although they are usually not as intrusive as cats like Siamese. They are reasonably active, they like to play and are extremely inventive in their games. They love to climb, and a sturdy cat gym and scratching post will be money well spent. Somalis are very bright, intelligent and inquisitive. Anything new will be examined, sniffed and inspected in detail, and your visitors will usually be greeted at length. Somalis' quiet voices are seldom heard.

Care

The Somali's semi-long coat can be maintained with the minimum of grooming. The

Red Somali

Fawn Somali

bone structure. The elegant paws are small and oval. The fairly long tail is plumed, broad at the base, and tapers to a point.

HEAD
The head is broad and moderately wedge-shaped, there is a slight nose break and the chin is very definite.

The almond-shaped eyes are slanting and have a lively expression. The relatively large ears are set low; they are broad at the base, tapering to a point. There are ear furnishings inside the ear, curling outward.

COAT
The Somali has a semi-long coat. The hair is noticeably longer and fuller on the haunches, the tail, the underparts and the ruff than it is on the rest of the body.

COLORS
The original Somali coat color is known as Usual in the United Kingdom and as Ruddy

in the United States and elsewhere. Over the years various other attractive colors have been developed from this original color, but the markings on the coat remain the same.

The back of the hind legs and the pads of the paws, for example, are always darker than the rest of the coat irrespective of the color. The nose is always brick-red with a darker outline.

All Somalis have striking ticking in their coat. On each individual hair the base color of the coat is interrupted by two or three bands of darker pigment, as found in the wild rabbit. The tip of the hair must always be dark.

The ticking should be as pure as possible, and barring or spotting in the coat (particularly on the neck and legs) are considered undesirable on the show bench. All colors may have a little white on the chin and whisker pads, but it certainly should not

Black Silver Somali

Silver
Silver Somalis are a separate color group among the Somalis. This variety is recognized everywhere in the world except in the USA. In Silvers the undercoat is always a pure silvery white. The markings include black (Black Silver), blue (Blue Silver), warm dark cream (Fawn Silver) and cinnamon (Sorrel Silver).

Good Silver Somalis are difficult to breed because they sometimes have undesirable tan patches and barring in the coat.

Special points

Somali kittens are born with dark coats that gradually lighten as they mature. It can sometimes take as long as two years for the final coat color to become established (see Chapter 7, Short-haired breeds, Abyssinian).

Nebelung (Long-haired Russian Blue)

The Nebelung is a semi-long-haired version of the Russian Blue. Semi-longhair Russian Blues had occasionally been seen in the past, but it was not until the mid 1980s that people started to take an interest in this variety.

The prime movers were in the United States, but with the fall of the Iron Curtain came the revelation that the variety had been bred in Russia, its country of origin, for some time. A number of individuals have since been brought to the West from Russia.

The gene for long hair had already been present in a number of bloodlines for a long time. The breed standard for the Nebelung (German for 'mist') is exactly the same as for the Russian Blue except, of course, for the length of the coat (see Chapter 7, Short-haired breeds, Russian Blue).

The Cat Fancier Association in the United States has not yet recognized the breed.

---

extend too far. Somalis without any white at all are rare. Somalis may sometimes have a grayish tinge to their coats. This is caused by the gray roots of the hairs. This gray cast will lose marks at shows. Regardless of the coat color, the eyes are amber, green or yellow and should be as clear as possible.

The colors described below are the most common, but Somalis occasionally occur in other attractive colors, including Chocolate and Tortie.

Ruddy
Usual or Ruddy is the best-known and most common coat color. The coat has a warm reddish-brown base, with black ticking. In Usual Somalis, the feet and the backs of the hind legs (boots) are always black.

Red
Red or Sorrel is another popular color. As in the Ruddy, the coat has a warm reddish-brown base, but the ticking, the soles of the feet and the backs of the legs are cinnamon rather than black.

Blue
Blue Somalis have become increasingly popular in recent years. The base color of the cat is light beige, and the ticking, the pads of the paws and the 'boots' are steel blue.

Fawn
Fawn Somalis are still relatively rare. The basic color of the coat is light cream, with darker cream ticking.
The 'boots' and the pads of the paws are a warm dark cream.

Nebelung

Bob Schwartz

Highland Fold
(Long-haired Scottish Fold)

The Highland Fold is the long-haired variant of the Scottish Fold.
The characteristic breed feature of both the Scottish Fold and the Highland Fold is the folded ears. This trait is brought about by a dominant gene which causes a defect in the cartilage. Unfortunately, this abnormality can also show up elsewhere in the body, which makes the breeding of these unusual cats far from easy. Highland Folds are placid, friendly and good-tempered.

History

The cat with the folded ears that was the progenitor of the Scottish Fold and the Highland Fold was born in Perthshire, Scotland, in the early 1960s. Word of this unusual animal soon spread and a number of cat breeders picked up the ear mutation and established it as a new breed of cat, the Scottish Fold.

Because the short-haired Scottish Fold was crossed from the outset with other breeds that were either long-haired or carried the gene for long hair, it is not surprising that in due course long-haired cats with folded ears were born. Long hair is caused by a recessive gene that can be passed on for generations.

At the beginning of the 1980s some American breeders found this variety so charming that they decided to breed it specifically. In the

United States the breed is simply referred to as the Scottish Fold Long Hair. Like Scottish Folds, Highland Folds are always mated with cats with normal ears in an endeavor to avoid other skeletal abnormalities.

Temperament

The character of the Highland Fold is essentially the same as that of the Scottish Fold.

Both breeds are friendly, good-tempered and equable. Highland Folds are placid cats, although they do enjoy a game from time to time. They get on extremely well with other cats, and seldom if ever have any problems with dogs. Their placid nature means that they are not easily ruffled, so they cope very well in more boisterous families. Highland Folds and children get along very well together. If things get too hectic for the

Highland Fold or Scottish Fold Long Hair

Bob Schwartz

Scottish Fold Long Hair kitten

Scottish Fold Long Hair

is not the case. If necessary, clean the ears with an ear cleaner especially designed for cats, which you can get from good pet shops and at cat shows. If you want to show your Highland Fold, you may need to bathe it a few days before the day of the show or clean its coat with unscented grooming powder. Massage a generous amount of powder into

Highland Fold, it is much more likely to remove itself from the situation than to show its claws. Highland Folds are fairly quiet cats with a soft, melodious voice.

Scottish Fold Long Hair

Care

The Highland Fold's coat does not need a great deal of grooming. When the cat is not shedding, you simply need to brush the coat every so often with a pig-bristle brush. The fur is inclined to become matted behind the ears, on the tail and in the groin area.

To prevent this, after the brushing session it is a good idea to comb these areas out gently with a wide-toothed comb.

During the shedding season, you can use a rubber massage mitt to remove the loose, dead hair from the coat quickly and easily, but do proceed with care since this useful grooming aid can damage the coat. Many people think that the Highland Fold's odd ears make it prone to ear infections, but this the coat and brush it out again almost immediately with a pig-bristle brush. The powder absorbs dirt and excess grease, leaving the coat clean and fresh-looking. Trim the claws with a pair of good clippers.

Physical characteristics

The breed standard for the Highland Fold is the same as for the Scottish Fold, with the exception of the coat. Like Scottish Folds, Highland Folds will be disqualified at shows if there are any abnormalities in the tail or elsewhere on the body.

COAT
The coat is semi-long and should be silky, not woolly. The mane should be well-developed and the hair on the flanks should be longer than that on the rest of the body.

Special points

See also Chapter 7, Short-haired breeds, Scottish Fold.

Semi-longhair American Curl

The long-haired American Curl has a typical long-haired house-cat coat, giving it a generally shaggy appearance. The soft fur is medium-length and seldom mats.
The combination of long hair and the backwards-curling ears gives this cat an interesting look.

History

The very first cat with the extraordinary backwards-curling ears was called Shulamith – a black stray taken in by the Ruga family in California. Shulamith gave birth to a litter of kittens, and two of them also had the curled ears. It was decided to establish the characteristic in a new breed, now known as the American Curl. Long-haired cats and cats

Semi-longhair American Curl

Bob Schwartz

that carried the gene for long hair were used in the breeding program, so long-haired kittens were quite common.

The breeders consequently decided to breed the long-haired American Curl too. The breed is presently found mainly in its country of origin and is still a relatively rare sight outside the United States.

Temperament

American Curls are extremely friendly cats. Very attached to people, they like to be the focus of attention.

They are also intelligent and inquisitive, and want to be involved in everything that goes on in the house. They love being stroked and petted, but can also be very playful and active – it all depends on their mood at the time. They are even-tempered and not easily put out, which makes them ideal pets for a family with young children. They get on extremely well with other cats and with dogs.

It is essential to give these cats enough opportunity to play and have a good romp. If you do not have a yard or outdoor run, make sure you have a good climbing post or cat gym in the house, because the cat will certainly make very good use of it.

The same applies to toys of all kinds. American Curls are not particularly talkative, but they will make themselves heard when they want to.

The American Curl has virtually no undercoat, so grooming generally presents no problems.

If you brush the coat once a week and then finish off with a fine comb, this will be enough to keep the cat looking smart. Clip the claws regularly to take the sharp tips off, and clean the ears if necessary with an ear cleaner especially designed for cats.

American Curls do not need any special ear care; the only thing to watch out for is that you do not bend the ears forwards because this can hurt the cat.

If you want to show your American Curl you can bathe it, but always use a special cat shampoo and do not wash it any later than three or four days prior to the show, so that the coat has time to recover.

Colorpoint Semi-longhair American Curl

BODY
The breed standard for the semi-long-haired American Curl is identical to the standard for the shorthair, with the exception of the length of the coat.

The American Curl is a medium-sized cat with a long, lean, elegant body. All parts of the body must be in proportion and the cat should be neither too stocky nor too slender. It can take two or three years for an American Curl to grow to full maturity.

HEAD
The head is slightly wedge-shaped and should be longer than it is wide. The ears are the American Curl's most distinctive feature; they feel less flexible than those of other breeds.

They stand upright at the corners of the head and curl smoothly backwards with the tips pointing towards the center of the base of the skull. An American Curl has a straight nose, a strong chin and large, walnut-shaped eyes.

COAT
The Semi-longhair American Curl's coat is fine, silky and soft to the touch; there is virtually no undercoat. There are also short-haired American Curls (see Chapter 7, Short-haired breeds, American Curl). There must always be ear furnishings curling outward from the inside of the ear, and small lynx tufts on the tips of the ears are considered to be a plus.

COLORS
This breed is found in every conceivable color and pattern. The most unusual combinations of markings and basic colors are possible. This lends the Curl great charm and also means that breeders can concentrate on breeding a cat of the best possible type. The eyes may be yellow or green; in Colorpoints they are always blue.

Cymric (Semi-longhair Manx)

The Cymric (pronounced 'kimrick') is the long-haired version of the Manx. Cymrics appeared regularly during the early years of the Manx breeding program, but surprisingly these attractive semi-long-haired cats were always overshadowed by the short-haired Manx. The Cymric is an essentially tailless cat but, contrary to what many people believe, this does not hamper the cat in any way. The Cymric can jump and climb like any other cat (think of the Lynx, the big cat with the short, stumpy tail). Cymrics are bred only in the 'natural' colors. They are friendly and affectionate, and their semi-long coat can be kept in good condition with the minimum of effort.

History

Manx cats have occurred for centuries on the Isle of Man, in the Irish Sea off Britain's west coast. No one knows for sure how these tailless cats came to be there, but the most likely explanation is that the first Manx cats were the result of a mutation. At the end of the nineteenth century, cat lovers from other parts of the world started to show an interest in the Manx and individuals were being

A thirteen-year-old Manx Long Hair or Cymric

Manx Long Hair (Cymric)

shown at cat shows in the United States and on the continent of Europe as early as 1890. The long-haired Manx was effectively ignored, although there had always been long-haired cats on the Isle of Man and long-haired kittens were exported in the early days.

Every so often long-haired kittens would be born to two short-haired Manx cats, but they were always regarded as a less attractive side-effect of serious Manx breeding.

Nevertheless, more and more fanciers started to appreciate the looks of the long-haired Manx. These cats were eventually given a separate breed name, Cymric, which is Welsh for 'Welsh.' Cymrics are crossed with one another and with Manx cats because, despite the different names, they are actually one and the same breed. In the United States, the breed is simply referred to as the Manx Long Hair.

Temperament

The Cymric's character is the same as that of the Manx cat. Cymrics are friendly, affectionate and extremely placid creatures. They are usually very trusting and will get on well with other cats and with dogs. You can teach Cymrics to retrieve pieces of paper and they can be trained to walk on a lead.

Despite their quiet, placid nature, Cymrics are exceptionally playful animals and will remain so as they get older. They are very good with children, and when they have had enough of a situation they will remove themselves to a quiet spot rather than lash out with their claws.

Although they lack the tail that people assume a cat needs to 'steer with', they are extremely accomplished climbers and scramblers. Cymrics are healthy cats that can live to an advanced age if they are well looked after.

Tailed Manx Long Hair

Care

The Cymric's semi-long coat is not prone to matting, so that all you need do is brush the cat regularly with a soft pig-bristle brush and then comb through the coat with a wide-toothed comb.

Manx Long Hair (Cymric)

If you want to show your Cymric, it may be necessary to groom the cat's coat more thoroughly.

You can bathe it a week before the day of the show, but you may prefer to clean its coat regularly with unscented grooming powder. Massage a generous amount of powder into the coat and brush it out again almost immediately with a soft brush until every trace of powder has vanished. The powder absorbs dirt and excess grease, leaving the coat clean and fresh-looking.

As with all cats, you should check the Cymric's ears regularly. Trim the claws occasionally with good clippers.

Physical characteristics

BODY
The breed standard for the Cymric is identical to the standard for the Manx, with the exception of the length of the coat.

Like the Manx, the Cymric is a sturdy, medium-sized cat with good bone structure. It is round and compact in form. The hind legs are clearly longer than the front legs, so that the back slopes upwards.

There are five different tail lengths. The completely tailless Cymric is known as a Rumpy; the Riser (or Rumpy riser) is a cat with no more than three coccygeal vertebrae (equivalent to the vestigial 'tail' or coccyx in humans) and no tail vertebrae; the Stumpy has a short stumpy tail; the Longie is a cat with a normal-looking but abnormally short tail; and the Tailed is a Cymric with a full-length tail.

The first three more or less tailless varieties can be shown; the last two are used in breeding provided they are good in terms of type.

HEAD
The head is round, with a sloping nose line. The ears are not set too high, they are broad and open at the base and they turn slightly outward. The eyes are large and round.

Manx Long Hair or Cymric

COAT
The Cymric has a semi-long double coat that feels very soft, thick and springy.

COLORS
Cymrics are only bred in natural 'farm cat' colors, in other words the colors found in ordinary European domestic cats: red, black and blue, possibly in a tabby pattern and with white markings, and pure white. All eye colors are permitted.

Special points

The gene for long hair occurs naturally in many of the Manx bloodlines. This means that there can always be a 'long-haired surprise' in a litter of Manx kittens (see also Chapter 7, Short-haired breeds, Manx).

195

Bob Schwartz

Semi-longhair American Bobtail

This cat is the long-haired variant of the short-haired American Bobtail. This is a relatively rare breed seldom seen outside the USA. The breed came about as a result of a spontaneous mutation and these cats are quite capable of fending for themselves if they have to. The fact that this cat has a short tail does not affect its mobility in any way, and the American Bobtail can climb and hunt with the best of them. In temperament it is the same as its short-haired counterpart. They are usually very friendly cats that soon develop a bond of trust with 'their' human family, but they can be shy with people they do not know. They get on extremely well with other cats and love to play with them. Because these cats are very active, it is well worth investing in a good scratching post and plenty of cat toys.

Physical characteristics

The standard for the semi-longhair American Bobtail is the same as for the shorthair. This is a medium-large to large breed and it may be two or three years before an individual is fully grown. For showing, judges like to see cats with a straight tail reaching halfway to the hock, although the tail may be slightly curved. The American Bobtail has a muscular body set on medium-length legs; the hind legs are always longer than the front legs. The paws are round and large. The semi-long coat is easy to care for. (See also Chapter 7, Short-haired breeds, American Bobtail.)

Japanese Bobtail

The semi-longhair Japanese Bobtail is essentially the same cat as the short-haired Japanese Bobtail, with the exception of the coat length. This breed is rarely seen outside Japan and the United States. These are friendly, sociable cats that get on very well with other animals. They are intelligent and inquisitive. The coat is not inclined to tangle, sheds remarkably little and is therefore quite easy to maintain.

Physical characteristics

The standard for the short-haired Japanese Bobtail also applies to this variety. Their short tails range from 5 to 8 centimeters (up to 4 inches) long and may be straight, curved or kinked – the latter give the effect of a pom-pom, particularly in the semi-longhair variety. The Japanese Bobtail is a medium-sized cat with a long, lean body and long legs with oval paws.

The wedge-shaped head has high cheekbones and the eyes are large and oval. The large ears are upright. The coat lies flat against the body and there is virtually no undercoat. The fur is soft and silky.

Semi-longhair Japanese Bobtail

Bob Schwartz

Japanese Bobtails occur in all colors, but the most popular cats are those that are predominantly white with a few clearly defined, deep colored markings. All eye colors are permitted in the Japanese Bobtail and odd-eyed forms are also found (see also Chapter 7, Short-haired breeds, Japanese Bobtail).

Munchkin, Semi-longhair

The semi-longhair Munchkin combines two separate factors: long hair and short legs. It is a medium-sized cat with short, straight, muscular legs and a wedge-shaped head.

History

The first Munchkins were two strays, Blackberry and Blueberry, found in the street in the state of Louisiana in the early 1980s. There had been reports of cats with extremely short legs elsewhere in the world prior to this, but nothing had ever been done about it. It was a different story with these American strays, one of which was used to create a new breed of cat–the Munchkin. Given the diversity of the breed's background and the fact that Munchkins can be mated with ordinary domestic cats (not pedigree cats!), it is not surprising that there is also a long-haired version of the Munchkin.

Since May 1995 it has been possible to show the breed as a shorthair and as a longhair at certain cat shows in the United States. However, the breed has not yet been recognized by the CFA.

Temperament

Like their short-haired relatives, Munchkins are friendly pets that get on very well with other cats and with dogs.
They are affectionate, enjoy human company and, with a little patience, can be taught to retrieve small toys and walk on a lead. Munchkins are lively by nature; they are active and playful extroverts.

The Munchkin can play and climb trees like any other cat, but its short legs prevent it from jumping very high.

A Munchkin will not be able to get up on the kitchen counter or the table without an intermediate stop on the way.

Care

The semi-longhair Munchkin needs little in the way of grooming. A weekly brush and comb session is all that is needed. Clip the claws regularly and clean the ears, but only when necessary, with a special ear cleaner for cats.

Physical characteristics

The breed standard for the semi-longhair Munchkin is the same as for the shorthair Munchkin except for the length of the coat (see Chapter 7, Short-haired breeds, Munchkin).

COAT AND COLORS
All coat colors, markings and patterns and eye colors are accepted.

Semi-longhair Munchkin

Bob Schwartz

10 Long-haired breeds

Persian Longhair

Without doubt the world's best-known and most popular breed of cat has to be the Persian Longhair. (Known as Persians in North America, in Great Britain they are referred to as Longhairs and each color is classed separately). Persian Longhairs are bred in an almost incredible variety of colors and patterns. Persian Longhairs have been and still are used all over the world in producing other breeds, including the Birman, the Selkirk Rex and the British Shorthair, to introduce new colors into these breeds, and in a number of cases to improve conformation and the shape of the skull. Because Persian Longhairs are extremely placid and affectionate, they get on well with other cats and with dogs. They are also extremely good with children. Grooming is probably the most important consideration for owners of a Persian Longhair. The Persian Longhair is the perfect pet for anyone who likes a cat with a gentle nature and also enjoys spending a lot of time caring for its coat every day.

History

The Persian Longhair most probably descends from the Angora cats of Turkey that

Cream Persian Longhair kitten

Left: White Persian Longhair

White Persian Longhair

sailors and merchants brought back with them from their trips to Turkey and Iran (Persia). For many years these semi-long-haired cats, known today as Turkish Angoras, were the darlings of Europe's aristocracy and even found favor at the French Court.

At the end of the nineteenth century, British cat lovers began to cross the elegant Angora (Angora was the old name for Ankara, the capital of Turkey) with other breeds, gradually creating cats of a heavier type and with a longer, thicker coat. These are the cats that developed into the world's most popular pedigree cat: the Persian Longhair.

Anyone who has ever seen a photograph or drawing of a Persian Longhair of the early days will know that they were very different creatures from the Persians bred today. The body has become much more compact, and the coat is longer and more profuse. The most obvious difference, however, is in the shape of the head and the length of the nose. The early Persian had a wedge-shaped head, whereas today's cats have larger, more rounded skulls.

The nose length remained virtually unchanged for years, but in recent decades fanciers have concentrated on breeding a Persian Longhair with an extremely short nose, and this has ultimately resulted in a cat with what is effectively a completely flat face. It is almost impossible to believe just how quickly these developments have taken place. A Grand Champion of the 1970s would not stand a chance in a show today.

Many cat lovers are unhappy about the breeding of short noses, because inexpert breeding can lead to problems including poor dentition, crooked jaws, respiratory problems and blocked tear ducts. Breeding a Persian Longhair of show quality is by no means an easy task and demands considerable skill and knowledge on the part of the breeders.

Temperament

Persian Longhairs are among the most placid of cat breeds. They are often described as phlegmatic and very docile.

They can spend hours lying in their favorite place in the house without taking the slightest notice of what is going on around them, at the same time appearing very conscious of their glamorous and aristocratic looks that so many people admire. Persians love being petted and stroked, and will take any amount of spoiling. The breed is generally friendly and good-tempered; these cats will very seldom show their claws. Fighting is simply not in the nature of these serene creatures. This is one of the reasons why they get on so well with other cats and with dogs.

Because they are almost imperturbable and impervious to stress, Persian Longhairs are usually good with children. They are rarely disturbed by a boisterous household, but if things do get too lively they will take themselves off to a peaceful spot, provided they are given the opportunity. Despite their tranquil nature, Persians will always be interested in a game. Unlike other cats, how-

A White Persian around the turn of the century

A Persian at a cat show around the turn of the century

200

ever, they will wait for you to invite them to play. As a rule they will not run and play of their own accord. This does not, of course, apply to the kittens: they are as playful and tireless as any other kitten.

Most Persian Longhairs have a very quiet voice that they rarely use. Compared with many other breeds they cope quite well with being left on their own, although they appreciate the company of another cat. The majority of Persians are perfectly happy indoors and show little inclination to go out, but this does depend on the individual cat and on whether it became accustomed to being outside at an early age.

Care

A very important part of owning a Persian Longhair is the care of the coat, but the eyes also need a considerable amount of attention. The coat is luxuriant and very thick, composed of long, soft hair that becomes tangled

During the shedding season your cat is likely to ingest a lot of hair during his daily grooming sessions.

Blue and White Bi-color Persian Longhair kittens

201

and matted very easily. If you fail to groom the cat for a couple of days, the coat will soon develop matted balls of fur that you will be unable to comb out without hurting the animal. Whether you keep your Persian Longhair as a pet or show it regularly, grooming is not something you can do when you happen to think about it, and you certainly cannot postpone it for as long as a week.

Fortunately, most Persians enjoy their daily grooming sessions, but there are some who absolutely hate it. This is not solely a question of the character of the individual cat. A good breeder will take care to get his or her kittens used to a daily brushing at an early age, so that they come to accept it as a matter of course and actually like it.

If you keep your Persian Longhair as a pet and do not intend to show it, it will be enough to brush the coat through daily, using a wire brush, and then gently comb any matted areas out once a week with a wide-toothed comb. The areas between the front and hind legs, the hair under the tail, the chest and the chin all need particular attention. Never pull hard on the coat; go about the job systematically and patiently. If the coat is dirty you can sprinkle in some unscented grooming powder, which will absorb the dirt and excess grease from the coat. You can get this powder from most large pet shops and at cat shows. After you have massaged the powder in, brush the coat carefully until not a trace of powder is left.

About once every three months you can bathe your Persian Longhair, but always use a good shampoo formulated specifically for cats. After a bath, the loose, dead hair that causes balls of matted hair in the coat can be brushed out more easily. Matted areas that simply cannot be removed in any other way can be very carefully cut out.

Persian Longhairs have considerable problems with watering eyes, which can

Black Mackerel Tabby Persian Longhair

White Persian Longhair

cause dark, unsightly tear marks in the creases of the face. It seems as though light-colored Persians suffer more from this problem, but this is simply because the marks show up more clearly. Try to prevent this dark discoloration as much as you possibly can, because in most cases neglected tear marks will cause permanent staining. Avoid this by cleaning the folds of the face and the hair around the eyes every day, using a soft tissue moistened with a special eye lotion for cats or with cooled, boiled water. Finally, you will have to clean the ears every now and then by massaging in a special ear cleaner and then removing the surface dirt with a cotton swab.

Broadly speaking, the grooming regime for show cats is the same as the routine for Persians kept as pets. They do have to be bathed more often, and the dead hair is plucked out of the coat by hand, a little at a time, every single day. According to the breed standard, a Persian Longhair's ears should be small. Exhibitors will consequently carefully trim or gently pluck the tiny hairs growing around the edge of the ear (not the ear furnishings in the ear!), because they make the ears appear bigger.

A show cat will also have to be powdered and brushed much more regularly to prevent any hint of matting and to keep the coat nicely loose, clean and full. The sharp points of a Persian Longhair's claws should be clipped off regularly with a good pair of clippers. Persian Longhairs are at their best in winter,

Cream Point Persian Longhair in profile

Black Persian Longhair

Black and White Bi-color Persian Longhair

Cream Persian Longhair

because they shed a significant proportion of their coat in spring and early summer. At this time of year you will need to make sure that your cat does not ingest too much hair during his own grooming sessions.

Physical characteristics

BODY

The Persian Longhair is a medium-sized to large cat with a sturdy bone structure. The body is compact, with a deep chest, muscular shoulders and a short, powerful neck. The legs are short and sturdy, and the paws are large and round. Tufts of hair between the toes are desirable. The tail is short, in good proportion to the body, with a slightly rounded tip.

HEAD

The head is round, massive and well-proportioned, with a broad skull and full cheeks. The forehead should be nicely rounded, and the short, very broad nose has a

Blue Persian Longhair

Black Classic Tabby Persian Longhair

Red Classic Tabby Persian Longhair

pronounced stop. The top of the nose should be on a horizontal line with the lower eyelids. The stop should be level with the center of the eyes.

The Persian Longhair has strong, broad jaws and a firm chin. The teeth should have a scissor action and preferably a complete bite. Viewed in profile, the chin, the top of the nose and the forehead should be in a straight vertical line. The small ears are broad at the base and rounded, with full ear furnishings in each ear. They are wide-set and placed low on the skull. The large, round eyes are set wide apart, and should be brilliant and expressive. The eye color, depending on the color of the coat, is copper, dark orange, green or blue; odd eyes are also permitted. Faults include ears that are too large, a nose that is too long, an indented bridge of the nose and almond-shaped eyes.

COAT

The Persian Longhair's coat is long and full, with a dense, fine, silky texture. This breed's characteristic coat forms a full mane and a bushy tail.

Persian Longhairs look their best in autumn and winter, because most of them will shed profusely in spring and early summer.

COLORS

The first Persians were white, a legacy of the white Angora cats from Turkey. Around 1900, the Blue Persian was very popular and – despite the fact that Persian Longhairs are now bred in an amazing range of coat patterns and unusual colors – these two colors still remain highly popular today.

Self colors

Self colors include white, black, blue, red, cream, chocolate and lilac. Longhairs with these coat colors have copper or orange eyes, but the White Longhair may also have two blue eyes or odd eyes. A self-colored Persian

Van/Harlequin Persian Longhair

Longhair (with the obvious exception of the White) may not have any white hairs or markings, and each hair should be the same color from the tip to the root in so far as possible. Ghost markings are quite common in kittens, and sometimes these vague tabby markings remain visible in the animal's coat as it gets older. These will lose marks at shows, although judges will turn a blind eye to them in the case of Cream and Red Longhairs, since it is extremely difficult to breed a completely self-colored coat in these colors.

It is also extremely difficult to achieve a true jet black and to keep it black, because this color can discolor to red or brown in places as a result of exposure to sunlight and damp. A self-colored cat with a silver undercoat is called a Smoke.

Particolors
Particolors are self-colored Persian Longhairs with white. There are two different varieties.

The best known is the Bi-color, which has a solid basic color with white markings that should be as symmetrical as possible. Bi-colors are found in all of the self colors.

207

Smoke Tortie Persian Longhair

Blue Point Persian Longhair

The other variety is the Tri-color, that has two basic colors, for example black and red, or blue and cream; here again, as in the case of the Bi-color, the white markings should be symmetrical. Tri-colors are also sometimes referred to as Tortie and White. In both varieties, the white should not cover more than one-third of the body, but not much less. It is difficult to breed a good Particolor Persian Longhair, because mating two Particolors will often result in kittens with too much white in their coats. This is why Particolors are usually crossed with self-colored individuals – and even this is no

Black Chinchilla Persian Longhair

Seal Point Persian Longhair ('old-fashioned' type)

Cream Point Persian Longhair

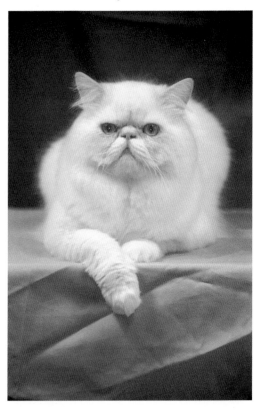

Seal Tabby Point Persian Longhair

Tortie Point Persian Longhair kitten

Red Point Persian Longhair

guarantee of the right proportion of white and the desirable symmetry in the markings. As well as the Particolors, there are Vans and Harlequins. In these varieties, the white in the coat predominates. All these cats should have copper or orange eyes. Cats that have different colored patches in their coats, but no white, are known as Tortoiseshells or Torties.

Tabbies

There are four different tabby patterns – ticked, mackerel (or striped), spotted and classic (or blotched).

Tabbies occur in black, red, blue and other colors, but whatever the color the markings have to be as clearly defined as possible. There are also Silver Tabbies, which we have

Blue Tortie Point Persian Longhair

Persian Longhair kittens at one week old

In a Shaded Chinchilla, approximately one-third of each individual hair contains pigment, but if only one-eighth of the hair is pigmented, the color is known as Tipped Chinchilla. These names are only given to cats with black pigment or colors derived from it such as blue, chocolate and lilac. These cats are extremely popular, in part because of their magnificent deep green eyes, their brick-red noses and the black 'mascara' lines around the eyes, nose and lips, which give them a film star glamour. Chinchilla and Shaded Silver Longhairs can produce kittens that have the parents' characteristic coat pattern, but not the silver color. In fact these are black tabby cats in which the pattern has been bred out by selection. They are referred to as Golden Persians.

If the pigment is red or cream and covers a third of the hair, the cat is known as a Cameo. Cats with coats this color where an eighth of the hair has pigmentation (in other words the

Black Shaded Silver Point Persian Longhair

looked at separately. With the exception of Black and Blue Silver Tabbies, all tabby cats should have copper or orange eyes.

Silvers and Goldens

Persian Longhairs with a silver undercoat, such as (Black) Silver Tabbies, Chinchillas, Cameos and Smokes, are very much in fashion.

The silver undercoat is caused by a gene known as an inhibitor, which inhibits the formation of pigment at the base of the hair, so that only the tip is colored. A distinction is made between self-colored cats and tabby cats with a silver undercoat.

When the inhibitor gene is present in a self-colored cat, this is known as Smoke. Judges at shows like to see approximately half of each hair with pigment. In the case of tabby cats the name varies depending on the amount of pigment in the coat and the color of the pigment.

tip of the hair only) are described as Shell. If a Persian has patches of red and/or cream, or has two different colors on its nose leather and/or paw pads, it is referred to as a Patched Tabby in the United States.

COLORPOINT

Colorpoint Longhairs are bred in all the colors found in the Siamese and, just as in the case of the Siamese, the contrast between the color of the body and the colored points (also known as the Himalayan pattern) should be as distinct as possible. Judges do not like darker shadows on the body, but in the Seal Point and Blue Point it is extremely difficult to breed cats with very little shadowing. Cats whose coats are a good, light color when they are young will inevitably develop darker shadows later as a result of exposure to the weather, minor injuries and licking the coat (saliva).

The breeding of good Red Points and Cream Points is also a problem. Because the tabby marking is always present as a dominant factor in these colors, even top judges find it

next to impossible to tell the difference between a self-colored Tabby Point and a Red or Cream Point without tabby markings. Colorpoint Longhairs are bred in Seal, Blue, Red, Cream, Chocolate and Lilac Point, with or without a tabby pattern. Tortie Points also occur, and recent additions include Silver and Golden Points.

At present, most Colorpoint Longhairs have light blue eyes, but breeders are working towards a dark blue.

Colorpoint kittens are always born white; the point color may emerge in a matter of days, although it usually takes a little longer.

Special points

If you are considering buying a Persian Longhair kitten, you would be wise to contact a cat association or a Persian Longhair breed club near you. They will be able to refer you to reliable breeders.

11 Breeds with unusual coats

American Wirehair

The American Wirehair is a breed that has developed from ordinary farm cats, one of which was born with an unusual coat that felt extraordinarily hard and wiry.

American Wirehairs are bred in all sorts of colors, apart from 'unnatural' colors like lilac, chocolate, fawn and cinnamon; the Himalayan pattern and the Burmese coloration are likewise not permitted in this breed. This breed is rarely found outside its country of origin.

History

The progenitor of all American Wirehairs was the result of a spontaneous mutation. In 1966, a red and white male was born on a farm in Verona, New York State. His litter brothers and sisters all had normal coats, but Adam was immediately noticeable because of his wiry hair.

An interested cat lover decided to take Adam and one of his litter sisters and mate them. Two of the resultant kittens had the same wiry coat texture as their father, so the

breeder started a breeding program to establish this unusual mutation. The progeny of the original mutation, Council Rock Farm Adams of Hi-Fi, are now in all areas of the United States. The mutation has not been reported in any other country thus far.

To prevent too much in-breeding, American Shorthairs were frequently used in the breeding program and cross breeding with this breed is still permitted. In 1978 the breed was officially recognized for championship competition by the American cat associations.

Temperament

In terms of character, the American Wirehair is very like the American Shorthair. Most American Wirehairs like their creature comforts and love to be petted and cuddled, but there are some who prefer to be out hunting. As a rule, American Wirehairs are intelligent, highly adaptable animals that will feel equally at home on a farm or in a top-floor flat.

The American Wirehair is a playful cat that loves to climb. If you are unable to let the cat work off its energy outdoors, it is a very good idea to invest in a good scratching post and cat gym. Generally speaking this breed gets on well with other cats and pets. They are also extremely good with children.

Care

The American Wirehair's wiry coat requires the minimum of grooming to keep it in good condition. During the shedding season you can remove loose, dead hair quickly and easily with a rubber brush, but use it carefully because it is all too easy to damage the coat with it. At other times of the year, brush the coat about once a week with a pig-bristle brush and follow up with a wide-toothed comb.

American Wirehair

Bob Schwartz

Left: Odd-eyed White American Wirehair

You can bathe an American Wirehair for a show if you wish, but be sure to do it at least a week before the show because it can take quite a while for the springy texture of the coat to recover fully.

Physical characteristics

BODY

The American Wirehair is a medium-sized, muscular cat; the bone structure is moderately heavy. The length of the sturdy legs should be in good proportion to the body.

American Wirehairs have compact paws and a medium-length tail with a rounded tip.

HEAD

The size of the head should be in good proportion to the rest of the body. The head is essentially round. The cheekbones are quite high. The eyes are round and should be medium-sized to large.

COAT

The American Wirehair has a short, curly coat with a coarse, hard texture; the hair on the underparts is somewhat softer. Each individual hair may be spiral-shaped or bent over at the tip.

The coat is springy, full and thick, and nothing like the coat of Rex cats, which is much shorter and finer in texture, with a far softer feel. The American Wirehair also has curly whiskers. The right coat texture is considered extremely important for show purposes.

COLORS

American Wirehairs are bred in the same coat colors as the American Shorthair.

German Rex

The German Rex is the earliest known breed of cat with a curly coat. There were reports of a stray with a curly coat in East Berlin as early as 1946, but it was not until the 1950s that German cat fanciers started to take a

Black Tortie German Rex

Bob Schwartz

real interest in the phenomenon. The gene that causes the curly coat in the German Rex is identical to that in the Cornish Rex. In terms of type, however, the breeds are very different. While the Cornish Rex is an elegant creature, the German Rex is a much sturdier, stockier cat that has more in common with a European house cat. It has an equable, tolerant nature. These cats make active but sensible companions that get on well with other cats.

Physical characteristics

The German Rex is a sturdily-built, medium-sized cat. It is closest in type to the European Shorthair. It has medium-length legs and round paws. The head is basically round, with well-developed cheeks. The ears are of medium size and the eyes are round. The characteristic breed feature is the fine, regularly waved coat. Like the Cornish Rex, the German Rex lacks guard hairs. The cat is bred in most of the colors and patterns found

214

in the European Shorthair and in domestic cats. The breed has not yet been recognized by the CFA, the largest association of breed organizations in the United States.

Cornish Rex

The Cornish Rex is one of the most striking breeds. These animals have a soft, curly coat that hardly sheds. They are very friendly and have delightful personalities.

History

The Cornish Rex is an English breed. The first Cornish Rex was born in Cornwall in 1950. This kitten turned out to be a spontaneous mutation. The kitten's mother had a normal coat, and the father was unknown.

Various breeders took an interest in this unusual kitten and decided to try to establish the gene that caused the curly hair in a new breed.

The Cornish Rex has been developed by crosses with domestic cats, British Shorthairs, Siamese and Oriental Shorthairs. This has resulted in an elegant, long-legged cat with a fairly long head. Over the years, two types of Cornish Rex have evolved–the European (English) type and the American type. They differ in conformation and in the shape of the head. The American cats are often smaller and leaner than the European

Black Tortie and White Cornish Rex

type. They also have longer legs and Roman noses. The European Cornish Rex is usually slightly bigger, the slender build is not quite so extreme, and the nose is straight.

Temperament

These friendly, affectionate cats love attention and like to be with people. They do not cope well with being left alone all day, so if you have to be out a lot you would be wise to get two of them.

The breed gets on extremely well with other cats and with dogs too. Cornish Rexes have an equable, gentle nature and seldom show their claws–one reason why they make such good pets for children. Their curiosity will lead them to get acquainted with every visitor, and they will be extremely friendly as soon as it becomes clear that the visitor likes cats.

Cornish Rex

Cornish Rex

The combination of intelligence, affection and curiosity means the Cornish Rex is a cat that you can teach all sorts of tricks, such as retrieving balls of paper or walking on a lead. The Cornish Rex has a placid temperament: these cats are not as active and playful as the Devon Rex, but they do nonetheless like to climb and play. A scratching and climbing post and a selection of toys will certainly not go to waste. These cats generally have no problem being indoor cats.

Care

A major advantage of the Cornish Rex is that the short, soft coat scarcely sheds at all. This makes the breed ideal for people who are allergic to cat hair–and these cats could also be the answer for anyone who hates finding hair on their clothes or their furniture. The Cornish Rex's coat is relatively easy to keep in good condition. A weekly brush with a soft baby brush, and an occasional comb-through with a fine-toothed comb is all that is needed. A rubber brush can be a useful aid in

Blue Cornish Rex

Blue Tortie Cornish Rex

Black Tortie and White Cornish Rex

Black Smoke and White Cornish Rex

removing the loose hairs from the coat, but do take great care because its over-enthusiastic use can cause irreparable damage to the coat. If you want to show your Cornish Rex it is a good idea to bathe the cat with a good cat shampoo several days before the day of the show.

Just before the cat is judged, you can go over it with a damp chamois – this brings out the waves in the coat. Trim the sharp tips off the claws regularly, using good clippers, and keep the ears clean with a special ear cleaner designed for cats.

Physical characteristics

BODY

The Cornish Rex is a small to medium-sized cat with a muscular body and fine bones. The legs are long and the paws are small and oval. The back should curve upwards slightly. The long, thin tail is slightly tapered.

Cream Cornish Rex

A particularly good Black Cornish Rex

COLORS

All colors are permitted in the Cornish Rex including Siamese markings – this variety is known as Si-Rex. At shows, more importance is attached to the quality of the coat than the color.

The most usual colors are self black and blue, with or without white patches and tabby markings in the coat, but Torties and predominantly white cats are also fairly common sights at shows. The eyes are green or yellow (except in the Si-Rex, when they are always blue) and should tone with the coat color.

Special points

The gene that causes the curly coat in the Cornish Rex is identical to that in the German Rex.

Black Cornish Rex

HEAD

The oval head is longer than it is wide, but it definitely must not be too long. Viewed in profile, the nose and chin should be in line. The Cornish Rex has a long nose: the American type has a Roman, slightly convex shape, the European type has a straight nose. The large ears are set high on the head but should not be too close together. The eyes are oval.

COAT

The coat is short and feels fine and beautifully soft. The Cornish Rex's coat is softer than that of the Devon Rex, because the Cornish Rex lacks the coarser guard hairs. In the ideal case, the curls form a dense, evenly waved coat rather reminiscent of a washboard.

This breed has no primary guard hairs at all. The whiskers and eyebrows are always crinkled. Bald patches in the coat or a bald tail are regarded as a fault on the show bench, but the kittens of this breed generally have thinner coats.

Devon Rex

This extraordinary cat evokes images of aliens from outer space and creatures out of fairy tales. The apparently fragile neck supports a broad triangular head with extremely large ears and very expressive eyes. The Devon Rex also has a remarkable curly coat and a very individual personality. Most people who have once owned a Devon Rex find it very difficult to get used to any other breed.

History

In 1960 a cat with a curly coat was born in the English county of Devon, to a feral cat living near a deserted tin mine and an adopted stray living nearby. Appropriately, the kitten was called Kirlee. Ten years earlier a similar cat had been found in neighboring Cornwall – this was the Cornish Rex named Kallibunker.

The newly-found cat and its descendants were initially crossed with Cornish Rexes because it was thought that the coat mutation was identical. It soon became clear that this was not in fact so, because the offspring of Kirlee and Kallibunker had straight hairs. Breeders decided to breed the second coat mutation separately and to name it after the county in which it had appeared.

The black male Kirlee was very unusual in type, with a quirky, pixie-like face and a moderately elegant body. This cat represented the first breed standard. The

Black Tortie and White Devon Rex

Devon Rex was then developed as a breed with the aid of many other pedigree breeds and ordinary domestic cats.

Temperament

The Devon Rex is an intelligent cat with a gentle, affectionate nature. These cats thrive on human company and do not cope well with being left alone. They are really happiest if they have people around them all day long, which means that it is not a good idea to leave a Devon Rex to spend its days in an outside run. The animal is quite likely to pine away and become ill due to loneliness.

Cats of this breed are very inquisitive and want to be involved in everything. Your groceries will be subjected to minute inspection and visitors will soon be made firm friends. Because they are so intelligent and so attached to the people they live with,

Black Mackerel Tabby Devon Rex

Devon Rexes usually get on very well with other cats, and most of them have no problems with dogs.

They are extremely good with children. Fighting is simply not in their nature. The fact that they hardly shed at all makes them ideal pets for many people. The Devon Rex's coat feels slightly harsher than the Cornish Rex's, because the Devon Rex has guard hairs.

Care

The Devon Rex's short, soft coat is easy to groom with a baby brush, or simply by stroking it often. Never use a hard brush, and always groom very gently since it is all too easy to damage the coat. Some hair will be shed during the shedding season – this can leave bald patches in the coat, but they will disappear later.

Blue Tabby Point Devon Rex

these cats can easily be taught all sorts of tricks, such as retrieving small toys, and they can be trained to walk on a lead. Devon Rexes remain very active and playful, even when they get older.
They love to jump and climb and will use your furniture for this purpose, which makes a good scratching and climbing post with several different levels a very wise investment.

Black Mackerel Tabby Devon Rex

Devon Rex

Devon Rex

Black Devon Rex kitten

An unusual characteristic of the Devon Rex is that it produces relatively large quantities of ear wax and is more prone to have dirty ears than other breeds.

This ear wax may sometimes be quite dark, which could lead you to suspect that the cat is suffering from ear mites, but this is usually not the case. You should massage a special ear cleaner into the ears regularly. Do not do this too often, however, because too much massaging will simply stimulate the production of more ear wax.

The excess production of sebum (skin grease) can also sometimes mystify the new owner of a Devon Rex, because it causes tarry particles and specks in the coat. Regular bathing with a good cat shampoo and careful grooming should be enough to control the problem to a significant extent.

The sharp tips of the claws should be trimmed off regularly with good clippers.

Physical characteristics

BODY

The Devon Rex is a fairly small cat with a slender, well-muscled body. The chest is deep and the slender legs are long in proportion to the body.

The hind legs are always longer than the forelegs. The paws are small and oval, and the tail is long, thin and tapering.

HEAD

A slender neck carries a wedge-shaped head with broad cheekbones, a strong chin and a short muzzle. There is a clear nose break and the forehead curves back towards the flat skull. The large ears are set quite low. They are broad at the base, tapering to a rounded point. The ears are covered with tiny, fine hairs. The large almond-shaped eyes are wide-set and slanting.

COAT

The coat is short, fine, wavy and soft, although it feels somewhat coarser than the coats of the German Rex and the Cornish Rex, because Devon Rexes have guard hairs as well as an undercoat. The whiskers and eyebrows are crinkled, fairly coarse and medium long. At shows, Devon Rexes with a smooth, untidy or partly bald coat will lose marks.

COLORS

All conceivable coat colors are permitted in this breed. Black and blue tortoiseshell (with or without white markings) are particularly common colors. Pure white cats and tabbies are widely found. There is also the attractive Si-Rex, with Siamese markings. The eyes are green or yellow (except in the Si-Rex, when they are always blue), and should tone with the coat. At shows, more importance is attached to the quality of the coat than to the color or the markings.

Special points

Because the Devon Rex sheds very little, it is sometimes recommended as a pet for people who are allergic to cats. It should be kept in mind, however, that some people may still have an adverse reaction – even to the Devon Rex – because dandruff can also be an allergen.

Devon Rex kittens usually have very sparse coats; the curly coat takes some time to develop. The Devon Rex is a relatively new breed, meaning that cross-breeding programs are still being undertaken with other breeds and domestic cats. Kittens from these crosses always have normal hair, but they can be used to breed Devon Rexes.

Selkirk Rex

If there is one cat above all others that is reminscent one of a teddy bear, it is the Selkirk Rex. This breed has a wonderfully soft, non-matting coat of loose curls.

This breed is quite popular in the United States but it is considerably less well-known in Europe, where very few of these cats are found.

History

In 1987 a kitten with a curly coat appeared in a litter of non-pedigree kittens born in the

Selkirk Rex

Selkirk Rex

Bob Schwartz

American Shorthair. This last breed is used to prevent the breed from developing a head shape that is too extreme.

Temperament

These cats are friendly, affectionate and gentle. They love human company and make excellent pets for children.

They get on very well with other cats and with dogs. Selkirk Rexes are active cats that love to play and climb. It would be wise to buy a good scratching post and cat gym, and provide plenty of toys in the shape of ping pong balls, pieces of paper and fur mice. If you accustom a Selkirk Rex kitten to a life indoors, there is a good chance that it will not want to go out when it is older.

Care

Selkirk Rexes may have long or short hair; neither type needs much in the way of grooming.

state of Wyoming. In contrast to other rex breeds, it was specifically decided to establish this new breed using only one other breed: the Persian Longhair. This was because the breeders wanted a type that was clearly different from the existing rex breeds, all of which were fairly elegant. Their efforts eventually resulted in a cat with a stocky, compact conformation, a round head and a heavy bone structure.

Unlike other rex mutations, the gene for the curly coat in the Selkirk Rex is dominant, so the first generation of Selkirk Rexes and Longhairs produced curly-coated kittens. Because the very first cat – a shorthair – was crossed with a long-haired cat, the breed has occurred with both long and short hair from the outset.

Because the Selkirk Rex is still in the process of becoming established, there are still regular crosses with the Persian Longhair, with the Exotic and occasionally with the

Unlike the Devon Rex and the Cornish Rex, this cat sheds in the same way as cats with normal coats. Outside the shedding season you can keep the coat in good condition by brushing it occasionally with a pig-bristle brush and following up with a wide-toothed comb.

In spring and early summer, when hair is being shed, the coat will require more attention. If you want to show your Selkirk Rex, you may need to bathe it a few days prior to the show.

Do not brush or comb the cat too thoroughly after a bath, because this could actually straighten the coat. On the day of the show you can damp the coat slightly with a plant mister to bring out the curls more clearly.

Trim the sharp claws regularly, using a good pair of clippers, and clean the ears if necessary with an ear cleaner especially formulated for cats.

223

Physical characteristics

BODY
The Selkirk Rex has a stocky build and the body is rectangular. This breed is very muscular and the bones are relatively heavy.

The legs are medium length and the paws are large and round. The thick tail has a rounded tip.

HEAD
The Selkirk Rex has a round, broad, medium-sized head with a clear stop at the bridge of the nose. The ears are set quite wide apart, are medium-sized and should have a rounded tip. The eyes are large, round and widely separated.

COAT
The double coat of both the long-haired and the short-haired Selkirk Rex is soft, plush and springy.

Kittens are born with curls, which disappear at around the age of six months. The curls reappear when the kittens are between eight and ten months old. It may take as long as two years for the coat to develop fully, so when kittens are shown the judges will pay more attention to the cat's build and type than to the curly coat. In an adult Selkirk Rex, the hair on the tail and around the neck will form more curls than the fur on the rest of the body.

The texture and profusion of the curls on the back may vary in response to the climate in which the cat lives and hormonal changes. Loose, springy curls, clearly distinct from one another, are highly desirable. The whiskers are always curled.

COLORS
All coat colors and patterns are permitted in the Selkirk Rex, as well as the 'natural' colors found in ordinary non-pedigree cats such as red, black, white and blue.

The Selkirk Rex also occurs with Siamese markings. At shows, the judges will be more concerned with the coat texture of an adult animal than with the color or patterning of the coat. All eye colors are permitted, but bright, expressive eyes are preferred

Special points

Because the gene that causes the Selkirk Rex's curly coat is inherited as a dominant factor, it is quite possible for two Selkirk Rexes to produce a litter containing one or more kittens with normal coats.

Poodle Cat

The Poodle Cat is a variety that has been created in Germany by crossing Scottish Folds and Rexes, with the aim of breeding a curly-coated cat with folded ears. The breed has not yet been recognized by any cat association. Poodle Cats are friendly, affectionate pets. They are bred in various colors, including colorpoint and the 'natur-

Poodle Cat

Bob Schwartz

224

al' colors found in non-pedigree cats. Coat care is similar to that of the other rexes, so it does not involve a great deal of grooming. Poodle Cats are rare and there are only a few breeders in Germany working on this breed.

Sphynx

The extraordinary appearance and virtually hairless skin of the Sphynx either fascinate or repel people. There seems to be no happy medium. Be this as it may, the breed is slowly but surely gaining in popularity and acquiring a growing circle of admirers. Aside from its virtually naked skin, the most obvious breed characteristics are the large paws with highly-developed pads, and the strikingly large ears. For cat lovers who are allergic to cat hair, this breed is a gift from heaven. However, if you are allergic to dandruff, the Sphynx will set off your allergy like any other cat.

Sphynx queen with kittens

The Aztecs are known to have had hairless cats like the Sphynx centuries ago, and they also bred hairless dogs (known as Xoloitzcuitlis). They still appear occasionally at shows in Europe and the United States.

The hairless cats were called Mexican Hairless. Because the gene responsible for the virtual absence of a coat in these cats is recessive, it may be passed down through many generations of cats before it comes to light. It is only when two cats that both carry the recessive gene for baldness mate that one or more of their kittens in the litter will betray the presence of the gene in their appearance.

It is believed that there are ordinary domestic cats in both Mexico and the United States carrying the naked gene of the Mexican Hairless. It is therefore not particularly surprising that two cats with normal coats

Sphynx

Paloma, one of the progenitors of the Sphynx line, at the age of sixteen

occasionally produce hairless kittens. The normal-coated American cat Jezebel was an important progenitor of the modern Sphynx bloodline in the United States.

The progenitors of the Sphynx lines in Europe were Punkie and Paloma. An animal lover found these two females roaming the streets of Toronto, Canada, at the end of the 1970s. The man wondered whether the kittens were suffering from some disease because they were practically bald, and got in touch with a cat breeder he knew, who soon established that these were Sphynx kittens. She sent the kittens to Hugo Hernandez in the Netherlands, because she knew that Hernandez had a Sphynx tom and was looking for queens. In the early stages the breeding base was not particularly broad, so the cats were crossed with both domestic cats and Devon Rexes, which are not dissimilar in

terms of type. These cats are still used on a limited scale in order to prevent in-breeding problems.

Although the breed has acquired international recognition, it is not one of the thirty-six breeds currently registered by the CFA.

Temperament

Sphynxes are affectionate and intelligent animals that soon establish a close bond with 'their' people. The character of the Sphynx has been described as 'part cat, part dog, part monkey and part child,' and this is certainly not far from the truth.

Sphynxes are very sociable and love human company, but they also get on very well with cats and other pets. Their laid-back nature means that they usually fit in very well in a lively family with children. You should never condemn the Sphynx to a solitary existence.

Black Mackerel Tabby Sphynx

226

Sphynx with kitten

They need a lot of contact and attention to keep them happy, and if they do not get it they will mope and in some cases quite literally die of loneliness. Sphynxes are so gentle and friendly that it is effectively impossible for them to act aggressively.

They are usually quite happy to be kept indoors, but do keep in mind that they are playful and active, and love to run and climb. Make sure that your cat has plenty of opportunity to play and work off its energy. A sturdy scratching and climbing post will generally be well used.

Some people say that the Sphynx has a higher constant body temperature than other cats, but this is not true. It only seems to be the case because the Sphynx's skin feels warm to the touch, but this is because of the absence of hair. For anyone who has never stroked a Sphynx, it feels something like the skin of a peach.

Care

It might appear that the Sphynx needs no grooming at all because it does not have a coat like other cats, but you should not underestimate the work that is actually involved in looking after a hairless skin.

Sphynxes perspire, just like people, and they produce a lot of sebum. If you never bathed

Sphynx

Sphynx kitten

Sphynx kittens

Physical characteristics

BODY

The Sphynx is a muscular, medium-sized cat with a deep chest and a barrel-shaped body. The length of the legs is in good proportion to the rest of the body and the hind legs are slightly longer than the front legs. The forelegs should be set wide apart and be a little bowed.

Sphynxes have medium-sized, oval paws with long toes, and the pads are noticeably thicker than those of other cats. The long, tapering tail should be in good proportion to the body.

HEAD

The Sphynx's medium-sized head is moderately wedge-shaped with rounded lines; it is slightly longer than it is wide. There is a gentle nose stop and the chin is firm. The muzzle should be strong and rounded, and may definitely not be pointed.

your Sphynx, it would start to smell after a while and the skin would feel greasy. Sphynx owners generally wash their cats twice a month with a neutral pH shampoo.

Fortunately, in contrast to many of the other breeds, most Sphynxes love a bath. Unlike the hairless dog breeds, Sphynx cats do not seem to be affected by UV radiation. They consequently do not suffer from sunburn, although the skin on the darker pigmented areas may become even darker. In summer and in hotter climates, most Sphynxes will develop freckles.

The Sphynx has a great many wrinkles, but generally speaking they do not require any special attention. Do be sure to clean the ears regularly with a special ear cleaner, however, and clip the claws every now and again. The skin usually remains supple, so there is no need to apply oil or other moisturizers. Most breeders in fact advise very strongly against the use of oil because it attracts unnecessary dirt that can block the pores.

Sphynx

Sphynx

The ears should be very large, and broad at the base. They must not be set on the top of the head, nor should they be placed too low. The Sphynx has large, somewhat slanting, lemon-shaped eyes, with the outer corners pointing to the outer edges of the ears.

COAT
The Sphynx is known as a hairless cat, but if you look carefully you will see that the cat's body is actually covered with very short, fine, downy hairs.
This down sheds quite readily. The hair may be slightly longer on the ears, muzzle, tail and paws (and on the scrotum in males), but at shows judges prefer cats that appear to be completely hairless. Kittens have very wrinkled skin, and judges like to see adult cats with as many wrinkles as possible, particularly on the head.
There is a limit to this, however, since too many wrinkles increases the risk of skin infection. Most Sphynxes have short, curly whiskers, but the total absence of whiskers is not considered a fault on the show bench.

COLORS
Sphynxes may be bred in every conceivable color and color combination; white patches are also permitted. Common colors include black tabby, tortoiseshell and particolor. The almost total absence of hair means that the color of the cat looks different from that of cats with normal coats.

It is often difficult for non-experts to tell what color the skin is. The eye color should harmonize with the color of the skin.

Special points

Because the breed is in the early stages of development, there are still regular out-crosses with suitable non-pedigree cats and with Devon Rexes.

The crosses with ordinary cats produce kittens with hair in the first generation; mated with Sphynxes, these cats can then produce bald kittens. When a Sphynx is crossed with a Devon Rex, the first generation may well be more or less hairless.

It is thought that the two genes for the Devon Rex (resulting in a reduction in hair) and the Sphynx (resulting in almost complete absence of coat) are related to each other.

Mexican Hairless, a photograph taken around the turn of the century

Glossary

The terms used in this encyclopedia of cats and in the world of cat fancy will not be familiar to everyone. Some of these terms are defined in this glossary. More detailed explanations can be found in Chapter 4.

Bi-color British Shorthair kitten

Agouti cat
Cats with tabby markings in their coats are known as agouti cats.

Bi-color
This literally means 'two colors,' and is used to describe cats with a self color combined with white. Ideally, cats with these markings have the self color over two-thirds of their body, with white markings arranged symmetrically over the rest. Bi-colors, Vans and Harlequins all come under the heading of Particolors.

Bi-color British Shorthair queen

Blotched
Another word for Classic (used for tabby cats).

Break
Another word for 'stop.'

Brown Tabby
Frequently used description for a black cat with tabby markings. This is actually incorrect, because the marking on the cat is black: Black Tabby would be more accurate in this case.

Calico
The American term for a Black Tortie and White cat.

Cameo
Tabby cats with a red or cream coat (phaeomelanin pigment) and an inhibitor gene, which causes the hair to be without pigment over two-thirds of its length, starting from the root, are described as Cameo.

Chinchilla
See Ticked.

Chocolate
Chocolate is derived from black. If the structure of the black pigment particles changes (mutates), the coat will be chocolate. Lilac is a dilute form of chocolate.

Cinnamon
This color is described as Sorrel or Red in the Abyssinian. Cinnamon occurs when the

Cameo Maine Coon

dilute form of red, and lilac is a dilute form of chocolate.

Dominant gene
Dominant genes are genes that always appear phenotypically, even if they are only present in single form.

Extremities
Legs, mask, tail, ears and the scrotum in males are referred to as the extremities. This term is generally only used in relation to colorpoints, because only the extremities are colored in these cats.

Fawn
Fawn is a dilute form of cinnamon. This color occurs if part of the pigment in the coat disappears as a result of a recessive gene. This makes the coat lighter.

Genetics
A thorough knowledge of genetics is crucial for any breeder. It is important to know that a

Blue Tortie and White Maine Coon

melanins that cause the chocolate color (the particles of pigment) mutate. This changes the structure of the melanins and the coat is cinnamon instead of chocolate. Fawn is the dilute form of cinnamon.

Classic
Another word for 'blotched,' used for tabby cats.

Colorpoint
Another word for the Siamese coat pattern, also known as the Himalayan pattern.

Dilute Calico
The American term for a Blue Tortie and White cat.

Dilution
The effect of a gene which causes some pigment cells (melanins) in the coat to disappear, so that the coat appears lighter. Blue is a dilute form of black, cream is a

Siamese have colored points (Cinnamon Point Siamese kitten).

cat can pass on not only the characteristics we can see (phenotype) but also carries invisible inherited traits in his genetic baggage (genotype) that he can hand down to subsequent generations.

Gene
The carrier of an inherited characteristic.

Genotype
The cat's genetic make-up is called the genotype. This can differ from the phenotype.

Ghost Marking
Vague tabby markings in non-agouti kittens are referred to as ghost markings. They usually disappear as the cat gets older, but they almost always remain in cats with phaeomelanin pigment (red and cream cats).

Golden
Occasionally two tabby cats, neither of which are purebred, will produce silver kittens with a sandy undercoat, in which the tabby markings are only very vague. These kittens are referred to as 'golden,' but in fact they are brown/black tabbies with indistinct tabby markings.

Harlequin
A cat with more than 90 percent white in its coat, with one or two colored spots on the top of the head (preferably not around the eyes), two or three colored spots on the body and a colored tail.

Heterozygotic
Not purebred. This term is used if the cat has two different genes for a particular characteristic. The cat's phenotype does not correspond to the cat's genotype (for example Dd).

Himalayan patterning
This is the marking seen in Siamese and Colorpoints. A particular gene causes the extremities of the cat to darken while the rest of the body remains lighter.

Homozygotic
Purebred. This term is used if both genes for a particular characteristic are the same (for example dd).

Inhibitor gene
The dominant gene that inhibits pigmentation of part of the hair shaft from the root upwards, causing a silver undercoat. This means that the cat's coat color only appears in the tips of the hairs.

In-breeding
The mating of very closely related cats (brother x sister, mother x son).

Black Shaded Golden Persian

Oriental Shorthair kitten with classic tabby patterning

Jowls
Strongly developed cheeks in adult males.

Kink
A defect in the bones of the tail which was formerly quite common in Siamese.

Lilac
Lilac is a dilute form of chocolate. This color occurs if part of the pigment in the coat disappears as a result of a recessive gene. This makes the coat lighter.

Line Breeding
Mating related animals together, for example grandmother x grandson, half-brother x half-sister.

Lynx Point
The American term for Tabby Point.

Mackerel
Another word for 'striped,' used for tabby cats.

Mutation
A spontaneous change in the genetic material that can be passed on to progeny. A great many viable cat breeds have come about as a result of spontaneous mutations, such as the Scottish Fold and the Munchkin, and mutations have also given rise to new coat colors.

Natural color
Natural colors are colors that occur in non-pedigree domestic cats, such as red, black and dilute forms of these colors, with or without white markings.

Pure white, tortoiseshell, a silver undercoat and tabby markings are also classified as natural colors.

Non-agouti cats
Every cat carries a dominant gene for a particular tabby pattern, but this pattern can only become evident if the cat also has a gene for agouti. Cats that do not have an agouti gene are sometimes referred to as non-agouti cats. These cats have a self-colored coat. Nonetheless most non-agouti kittens will have vague tabby markings (ghost markings) in the coat, which will disappear as they get older. Cats with phaeomelanin pigment (red and cream cats) almost always retain these ghost markings.

Non-natural colors
Colors and markings never seen in ordinary domestic cats. These include Burmese, Siamese and Tonkinese markings, and colors like chocolate, lilac, cinnamon and fawn.

Odd-eyed White Oriental Shorthair

Odd-eyed
Cats with different colored eyes.

Oriental conformation
A very lithe, lean, elegant body shape typically seen in Oriental type cats.

Particolors
A group of cats that have a self basic color and a certain amount of white in the coat. The Particolors include Bi-colors, Tri-colors, Vans and Harlequins.

Patched Tabby
Term used in the United States for Tabby cats with patches of red and/or cream or with two different colors on its nose leather and/or paw pads.

Phenotype
The outward appearance of the cat.

Points
Dark colored extremities as seen in Siamese and Colorpoints.

Ruddy Somali

Recessive gene
Recessive genes are genes that can only appear phenotypically if the kitten receives them from both parents.

Ruddy
The term used in the United States and elsewhere for the original Abyssinian and Somali color known as Usual in the United Kingdom.

Seal
Dark brown coloration, used primarily with reference to Siamese and Colorpoints.

Self
Term used for a solid-color (non-agouti) cat.

Shaded
Term used for tabby cats with black, lilac, blue or chocolate coats (eumelanin pigment), in which approximately two-thirds of each hair is unpigmented from the root as a result of the inhibitor gene.

Shell
Tabby cats with a red or cream coat (phaeomelanin pigment) and an inhibitor gene, which causes the hair to be without pigment over seven-eighths of its length, starting from the root, are described as Shell. Because only the very tips of the hair are colored, the cat looks virtually white.

Smoke
When a non-agouti cat has a silver undercoat as a result of the inhibitor gene, it is referred to as Smoke, in which case one-half of the hair length is colored at the tip.

Stocky
A short, compact body shape specified for the British Shorthair and other breeds.

Stop
An indentation in the nose, particularly obvious in Persian Longhairs. Also known as a nose break.

Tabby
There are four different tabby patterns in domestic cats: ticked, mackerel, spotted and classic. In the United States, in addition to the mackerel and spotted classic tabbys, there

Black Tortie Persian Longhair

(eumelanin pigment) in which an inhibitor gene causes the hair to be without pigment over seven-eighths of its length, starting from the root. Because only the very tips of the hair are colored, the cat looks virtually white. Tipped cats are also referred to as Chinchillas.

Torbie
Old-fashioned name for Tortie Tabby.

Tortie (Tortoiseshell)
A coat pattern consisting of small, irregularly shaped patches of color. Torties may have black, blue, chocolate or lilac as the basic color.

Tortie Tabby
Tortie Tabbies have both a tortoiseshell and a tabby pattern in the coat.

Usual
The term used in the United Kingdom for the original Abyssinian and Somali color known as Ruddy in the United States and elsewhere.

Black Chinchilla Persian Longhair

is a classification known as the patched tabby.

Ticked
One of the four tabby patterns in which each individual hair has two or three darker bands. Ticked is also referred to as the Abyssinian tabby pattern because it is typical of Abyssinians, but it also occurs in other breeds. Ticked is not a classification applied by the CFA in the United States.

Tipped
Tipped is a term used to describe Black, Blue, Cinnamon, Chocolate and Lilac Tabbies

This Maine Coon has both tortoiseshell and tabby markings in its coat.

Van pattern (Europe)
The name for the coat pattern of a white cat with two patches of color on the head, a colored tail, and a small colored patch on the body.

Van pattern (USA)
The name for the coat pattern of a white cat with two patches of color on the head and a colored tail.

Domestic cat with black and white Van pattern

Index

Acknowledgements

The author and publisher would like to thank the following people for giving us their time and making their cats available:

Ms Balemans; Olga van Beek; Ms H. Berntrop; Ms H. Bok; the v.d. Bos family; Cath Brandt; Jan Deetman; A. van Dongen; A.M.A. Duin-Uringer; Annelies Edeling; A. van Eeuwijk; Marit van Eewijk; Andrea van Elmpt; Anne and Werner Friedhoff; Leonie van Gent; Diane Goossens; Sabine Hamburger; the Harks family; Marga Harms; Caroline Harmsel; Elly and Peter van Hecke; Marg Henderson; Ms H. Hendriks; Ms T. Hinten; the den Hollander family; Hans Hothinrichs; Irma Jeelof; Ronald Kamphorst; Jose Kerkhoffs; J. and R. Kern; the der Kinderen family; Ms E. Kwappenberg; the Linnenbank family; Peter and Yvonne van Lissum; André and Caroline Maas; Yvonne Maas; Mariska van der Meer; Marvin Miseroy; Jaco and Bianca Muriel; the Nettenbreijer family; I. van Oorschot; the Den Ouden family; Jaap and Wil Ouwehand; Sebastian and Carin Poos; Marco Pullens; Aad Quast; the Van Rooij family; the Rulke family; Esther Rulke; Suzanne Ruthsatz; Jet Sluijters-Hamburger; Mimy Sluiter; Ab and Joke Smid-Smit and family; Els Smits; Eveline Smits; Ms Soetens; Marielle van Son; the Stigter family; Richard van Veen; the Verhoef family; Kai Verlaan; Claudia Wagterveld; Gisele Wal; Leslie Wal; Marga Wal-Lindeboom; W. Wallenta; Robin van Wees; Twannie van Wees; Mieke van Wees-Levendig; A.E. Wilmering-Keizer; Ms H. Wirahadiraksa-Zaagmans; Bea v.d. Woude; Annet Wouters, Judith Zuurveld; Cees and Marion Zwart.

A particular debt of gratitude is owed to Marga Harms, Marvin Miseroy and Jan Deetman, whose help we were always able to count on in preparing this book for publication. And special thanks, too, to the following people, who really put themselves out to help in one way or another: Ms H. Bok; Andrea van Elmpt; Genoveva Giepmans and Ivar Duppen; Caroline Harmsel, Terri J. Harris (USA), Jose Kerkhoffs, Ab and Joke Smid-Smit, Eveline Smits and Leslie Wal.

The author and publisher would also like to thank all the photographers for their additional material, particularly Bob Schwartz (Italy), without whose contributions several breeds could not have been illustrated so comprehensively; also the Friedhoff family (Belgium), Genoveva Giepmans and Ivar Duppen (Netherlands), the Kern family (Germany) and Eveline Smits (Netherlands) for making photographs and slides available.

Special thanks go to Mimy Sluiter, whose expertise in matters feline made her an invaluable editor. Thank you, Mimy!